Anonymous

The Poppy in China

Anonymous

The Poppy in China

ISBN/EAN: 9783744691994

Printed in Europe, USA, Canada, Australia, Japan

Cover: Foto ©Thomas Meinert / pixelio.de

More available books at **www.hansebooks.com**

IMPERIAL MARITIME CUSTOMS.

II.—SPECIAL SERIES: No. 13.

OPIUM:

HISTORICAL NOTE,

OR

THE POPPY IN CHINA.

PUBLISHED BY ORDER OF

The Inspector General of Customs.

SHANGHAI:
PUBLISHED AT THE STATISTICAL DEPARTMENT OF THE INSPECTORATE GENERAL OF CUSTOMS.
AND SOLD BY
KELLY & WALSH, LIMITED: SHANGHAI, HONGKONG, YOKOHAMA, AND SINGAPORE.
LONDON: P. S. KING & SON, CANADA BUILDING, KING STREET, WESTMINSTER, S.W.

1889.

TABLE OF CONTENTS.

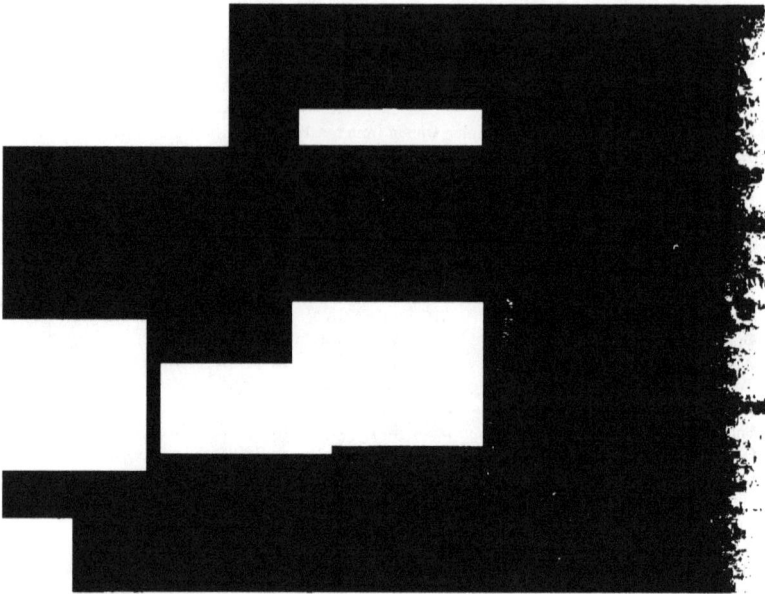

been

lished

tory.

PIUM: HISTORICAL NOTE,

THE POPPY IN CHINA.

1°. --

Poppy was cultivated very early in Italy is clear from
ros, who, in his account of TARQUIN, mentions it in a way
of the last of the Roman Kings it was commonly sown in
in a city of Etruria, devising means to betray it to
losing the confidence of the people, who believed father
opeless alienation, he having come to their city with woun
aid had been inflicted by his father as a punishment.
father for advice. The father* took the envoy into his g
the tallest Poppies. SEXTUS TARQUINIUS knew what th
the death or removal from the city of all the chief in
ading the remainder to submit to his father's rule.

is also alluded to in HOMER as a garden flower. He de
HECTOR as missing him, but striking in the chest anoth
ds, "Just as a Poppy in a garden hangs on one side
d with the dew of spring, so he bent on one side his
t."† The first mention of Poppy juice is by HIPPOCR

---

guis, credo, dubiæ fidei videbatur, nihil voce responsum est. Rex, velut
sequente nuntio filii: ibi, inambulans tacitus, summa papaverum capita

† μήκων δ' ὡς ἑτέρωσε κάρη βάλεν, ἥτ' ἐνὶ κήπῳ,
καρπῷ βριθομένη νοτίῃσί τε εἰαρινῇσιν·
ὣς ἑτέρωσ' ἤμυσε κάρη πήληκι βαρυνθέν.—*Iliad*, viii, 306-8.

calls it ὀπὸς μήκωνος. From ὀπός, "juice," was formed ὄπιον in Greek, and *Opium* in Latin. Μήκων is the Greek name of the Poppy. HIPPOCRATES lived in the fifth century before Christ. He was famous as the founder of Greek medical literature, and to him certainly the virtues of the Poppy were known.

In VIRGIL we find the Poppy described as pervaded by lethean sleep ("Lethæo perfusa papavera somno."—*Georg.*, i, 78), and he sometimes speaks of the "lethean Poppy" or the "sleep-giving Poppy" ("soporiferumque papaver."—*Æneid*, iv, 486). He borrowed from Greek mythology, according to which the waters of the river Lethe, which flows through the regions of the dead, cause those who drink of them to forget everything, as is said also to have been the case with the lotus-eaters of HOMER. The Poppy is in VIRGIL connected not only with the mythology of the world of the dead, but with the worship of CERES. This goddess is represented as holding the Poppy in her hands. Conjecture has been busy in attempting to account for this, and it has been supposed that it was because the Poppy grows wild in corn-fields in European countries, or because the seeds of the white Poppy were eaten as food to give an appetite, CERES being thought of by the ancient mind as the bountiful giver of food. To the ancient imagination, however, it would be quite enough to think of the Poppy as the prettiest of the flowers which grow up wild in the midst of wheat, and on this account to dedicate it to the service of the goddess of the wheat-field. When, in the first Christian century, PLINY wrote his *Natural History* (20, 18 (76), 199) and DIOSCORIDES his *Materia Medica*, the word "Opium" was already introduced, and the sleepy effects of it were everywhere known.

2°.

Poppy among Arabs.

The Arabians of the Caliphate studied Greek medicine and practised it. Opium became well known among them by its Greek name, which took the form *afyûn*, through the Semitic habit of changing *p* to *f*. In Persia it appeared with the same form *(afyûn)*, interchanged with *abyûn* and *apyûn*, which latter became, as will be seen, the parent of the Chinese name *ya-pien* (阿 扁). Both the Arabs and the Persians had national names for the Poppy: the Arab called it *khash-khash*, and the Persian *kôknâr*. Hence we may gather that the Poppy was anciently known as a garden flower as far eastward as Persia, while its medical applications were made by the Greeks.[*]

In the times of the Caliphs the Arabs began to visit China,[†] especially after the founding of Baghdad, A.D. 763, and became traders in drugs, precious stones, brocades, rose water, and such things. Previous to the T'ANG dynasty the Poppy was apparently unknown to the Chinese botanists and physicians, and when it was brought to them their attention was drawn to the form of the heads which enclosed the seeds, then used in making a soporiferous decoction according to the directions of the Arab doctors; consequently they invented names for it, based on the appearance of the Poppy heads. The seeds looked like millet seeds, if not in colour, at least in shape, and therefore they called the heads *mi-nang* (米囊), "millet bags."

The Arabs in China.

The early arrival of Arabs by sea at Canton may be illustrated by the following extract from the *Pan-yü-hsien-chih* (番禺縣志):—"In the T'ANG dynasty, on occasion of the opening of trade with Foreign ships, the Mahommedan King MAHOMET sent his mother's brother from Western countries to China to trade. He built a tomb and monastery, called respectively *Chien-kuang-t'a* (建光塔) and *Huai-shêng-ssŭ* (懷聖寺). Soon after the monastery was completed he died, and was buried in the tomb [still existing outside the North Gate], in accordance with his intention."

The Arabs at Canton.

3°.

In the reign of T'ANG MING HUANG, in the first half of the eighth century, an author named CH'ÊN TS'ANG-CH'I (陳藏器), in a work which he calls *A Supplement to the Pên-ts'ao* (本草拾遺), quotes from an earlier writer, SUNG YANG-TZŬ (嵩陽子), a statement that "The Poppy has four petals. It is white and red. Above them is a pale red rim. The seeds are in a bag, which is like one of those arrow-heads which have air-holes to make a sound as the arrow cuts through the air. Within there are seeds like those of millet."

First mention of cultivation of the Poppy in China in the eighth century.

[*] Opium is also mentioned in the Jerusalem *Talmud* (seventh century), Aboda Zarah, ii, 40 (ophyón, יצ׳טיף), as being a dangerous medicine.

[†] China in the early HAN dynasty opened Foreign trade by way of Cochin China. Under the WEI dynasty international trade was established at certain points on the border between North and South China. In the SUNG dynasty, A.D. 971, a Superintendent was appointed at Canton, Hangchow, and Ningpo, to overlook Foreign trade. Earlier than this we read of an officer called *Shih-po-ssŭ* (市舶司), appointed to Canton to superintend Foreign trade, as the title implies. This was in the T'ANG dynasty.

At this time, early in the eighth century, the Arabs had been trading with China for at least a century, for MAHOMET's death occurred A.D. 632, and that of his uncle not long afterwards. It was easy for the Poppy to be cultivated with the jasmine and the rose everywhere throughout the country. We know, indeed, from the *Nan-fang-ts'ao-mu-chuang* (南方草木狀), a work which dates from the beginning of the fourth century, that the jasmine and the henna, plants which must have come with the Arabian commerce, were already in China when that book was written. But the first distinct mention of the Poppy is in the work of CH'ÊN TS'ANG-CH'I.

Second mention. In the work on trees, called *Chung-shu-shu* (種樹書), written by KUO T'O-T'O (郭橐駝), it is said that "The Poppy, *ying-su* (罌粟), if sown on the 9th of the 9th month or on the 15th of the 8th month, the flowers will be large and the heads full of seeds." This passage occurs in the *T'u-shu-chi-ch'êng* (圖書集成).* The author's biography was written by LIU TSUNG-YÜAN (柳宗元), and we therefore know that he was living in the latter part of the eighth century. He resided near the capital, in Shensi. From this it must be concluded that the Poppy was then cultivated in the neighbourhood of what is now Si-an-fu (provincial capital of Shensi).

Early poem on the Poppy. The poet YUNG T'AO (雍陶), a native of Ch'êng-tu-fu, in Szechwan, in the closing years of the T'ANG dynasty, wrote a poem, entitled *A Poem on leaving a winding Valley and approaching my Western Home*. It says, "Passing the dangerous staircase I issued from the winding defile of the Pao Valley. After travelling across all the intervening plains and rivers I am now near my home. The sadness of the traveller in his journey of 10,000 *li* is to-day dissipated. Before my horse I see the *mi-nang* flower." This short poem shows that at the time when it was written the Poppy was cultivated near Ch'êng-tu-fu.

4°.

The two Arab travellers. From about 756 to 960, a space of two centuries, little is said in Chinese books of the Arabs; yet at that time two Mahommedan travellers came to China and wrote accounts of what they saw and heard. Recently their works have been

---

* Kindly lent from the Russian Legation Library, Peking.

translated into European languages. This shows that the Arabs did not cease during this interval to visit China. Information in regard to the medical qualities of the Poppy would be originally furnished to the Chinese by the Arabs; it is on this account that in the *Pên-ts'ao* of the K'AI PAO period (A.D. 968 to 976) the Poppy is introduced as a healing plant.

5'.

In the year 973 the Emperor SUNG T'AI-TSU gave an order that LIU HAN (劉 翰) and a Taoist, MA CHIH (馬 志), with others, nine in all, should prepare the medical work known as *K'ai-pao-pên-ts'ao* (開 寶 本 草). In this the Poppy is called *ying-tzŭ-su* (櫻 子 粟), and it is stated that "Its seeds have healing powers. When men have been taking the stone * that confers immortality, feel it powerfully operating, and cannot eat with appetite, they may be benefited by mixing these seeds with bamboo juice boiled into gruel and taking this."

The Poppy enters the Chinese *Pharmacopœia.*

The name *ying-su* here used, and previously by the earliest T'ANG dynasty authors on this point, means "jar millet," from the resemblance of the Poppy head to the kind of jar which the Chinese call *ying.*

Among the poets of this period were two brothers named SU; one was the celebrated SU TUNG-P'O (蘇 東 坡). In a poem of his occurs the following passage :— "The Taoist advises you strongly to partake of the drink called *chi-su-shui* (鷄 蘇 水). The boy may prepare for you the broth of the *ying-su.*"

Poem of Su Tung-p'o.

The brother, named SU CHÊ (蘇 轍), wrote a poem which he called *A Poem on the Cultivation of the Medical Plant "Ying-su," or Poppy* :—

Poem of Su Chê.

"I built a house on the west of the city. The ground in the centre was laid out in rectangular divisions. Where the windows and doors left a space, firs and bamboos helped to fill up the vacancy. The thorny bushes were pulled up, and a garden made to grow good vegetables and other plants. The gardener came to me to say, 'The *ying-su* (Poppy) is a good plant to have.' It is called *ying* because, though small, it is shaped like a *ying* (jar); it is called *su* because the seeds are

* This statement shows that at that time there prevailed an extensive use of mercury, taken under the idea that it would prolong life, and that the effects were found to be very injurious.

small and look like *su* (millet). It is sown with wheat and ripens with panicled millet—*chi* (穄), *Panicum miliaceum*; when growing it may be eaten like the vegetables of spring. Its seeds are like autumn millet. When ground they yield a sap like cows' milk; when boiled they become a drink fit for BUDDHA. Old men whose powers have decayed, who have little appetite, who when they eat meat cannot digest it, and when they eat vegetables cannot distinguish their flavour, should take this drink. Use a willow mallet and a stone basin to beat it. Boil it in water that has been sweetened with honey. It does good to the mouth and to the throat. It restores tranquillity to the lungs and nourishes the stomach. For three years the door has been closed, and I have gone nowhere and come back from nowhere. I see here the Hermit of the Shade (a Taoist priest) and the long-robed Buddhist priest; when they sit opposite I forget to' speak. Then I have but to drink a cup of this Poppy-seed decoction. I laugh, I am happy, I have come to Ying-ch'uan, and am wandering on the banks of its river. I seem to be climbing the slopes of the Lu Mountain in the far west."

Notes on the poem.

There is a small river in the province of Anhwei which is called Ying-shui. The city mentioned was on the banks of that river, which is famous in history. The mountain called Lu-shan is in Western China, on the north of the celebrated O-mei-shan. The poet went to live at Ying-ch'uan when he was old. As a boy he had lived with his brother near the Lu Mountain.

6°.

Materia Medica of the eleventh century by Su Sung.

The Emperor JĚN TSUNG, of the SUNG dynasty, about the year 1057, ordered the compilation by SU SUNG (蘇 頌) and others of the work known as *T'u-ching-pén-ts'ao* (圖 經 本 草). The magistrates of all cities were ordered to supply information on all medical plants in their vicinity, according to the method before employed in preparing the previous work, called *Ying-kung T'ang Pén-ts'ao* (英 公 唐 本 草), made in pursuance of an order given by the Emperor KAO TSUNG, in the T'ANG dynasty, to the Prince named YING KUO-KUNG (英 國 公). In this work it is said

Cultivation of the Poppy mentioned.

by SU SUNG that "The Poppy is found everywhere. Many persons cultivate it as an ornamental flower. There are two kinds, one with red flowers and another with white. It has an odour not very agreeable. The fruit is like a flower vase, and contains very small seeds. Gardeners manure the land for the Poppy every other year. The seeds are sown in the 9th month. In the spring they are, if thus manured, seen growing with great vigour; otherwise they will not thrive, and if they grow at all they are weak and slender. When the capsules have become dry and yellow, they may be plucked."

He also says that "In cases of nausea and vomiting a drink made from Poppy seeds in the following manner will be found serviceable. Three-tenths of a pint of the seeds of the white Poppy, three-tenths of an ounce of powdered ginseng, with a piece 5 inches in length of the tuber of the Chinese yam, are to be cut and ground fine. Boil it, adding $2\frac{3}{10}$ pints of water. Take of this six-tenths of a pint, and add to it a little syrup of raw ginger with fine salt. It should be mixed well and distributed into doses, which may be taken early or late, and no harm will follow from taking other kinds of medicine at the same time." Medical use of Poppy seeds.

The biography of this writer in the *History of the Sung Dynasty* says of him that he was a man of large mind, who would not take part in quarrels. He held to the rules of politeness and the laws of the State. Though high in station he lived like a poor man. From the invention of writing downwards, whatever there was to read and to learn in classics, histories, and the works of various authors, together with diviners' books, the 12 musical tubes, astronomy, astrology, mathematics, and medical botany, there was nothing with which he was not familiar.

In regard to what kind of Poppy is meant by SU SUNG, writing in the eleventh century, it may be well to refer here to the statement made by the German traveller KÆMPFER, who towards the end of the seventeenth century was attached as physician to the Embassy sent to Persia by the King of Sweden. He says that the Poppy from which Opium was then manufactured in that country was the white Poppy. It becomes plain, then, that in the time of SU SUNG, though the name of Opium had not yet appeared in books, yet the plant that was able to produce it was commonly known. The celebrated English botanist LINDLEY says that the Poppies from which Opium is made are those with red and those with white flowers. The white variety of *Papaver somniferum*.

7.

Twelfth century
use of seeds to
counteract the
effects of mercury.

At the beginning of the twelfth century, in the reign of HUI TSUNG, one of the Court physicians, named K'OU TSUNG-SHIH (寇宗奭), compiled a work called *Pên-ts'ao-yen-i* (本草衍義). In it he says that the flowers of the Poppy are in some kinds extremely abundant in their leaves, and that the number of seeds in the heads is beyond computation. "They are in size like those of the *t'ing-li* (葶藶),* and white in colour. The seeds are cooling in their nature ; if taken in good quantity they are beneficial for such affections as diarrhœa, and act favourably on the bladder. Those who have been taking cinnabar, if they have them ground and boiled with water, adding honey, and prepared in the form of broth, will find them beneficial in a high degree."

First use of cap-
sules in twelfth
century.

In the botanical section of the *T'u-shu-chi-ch'êng* the following extract is found, taken from the work *Shan-chia-ch'ing-kung* (山家清供), by a SUNG dynasty medical writer named LIN HUNG (林洪), who, from his language implying the use of the capsules of the Poppy with the seeds, we must suppose to have belonged to the SOUTHERN SUNG. He is speaking of what he calls Poppy-milk fish, by which is meant the juice hardened into cakes and taking the shape of fish. "Take Poppy heads, wash them well, and grind out their juice. First place some meal in a jar, covering the bottom. By means of a gauze bag filter the Poppy milk upon it, removing the portion that floats above and allowing the thicker part to remain. Place it in an iron pan and let it boil for a little. Sprinkle rapidly some weak vinegar on it, and take it up from the pan into the bag and press it into a cake. It should then be placed in such a covered pan as is used for steaming macaroni and the like, and there be well steamed. It is then to be sprinkled with a solution of red leaven, steamed again for a short time, taken out, and made up in cakes shaped like fish."

Another poem on
the Poppy.

A poem of HSIEH K'o (謝翱), written in the SUNG dynasty, is found in the work known as *Kuang-ch'ün-fang-p'u* (廣羣芳譜). "There seem to be tiny spots

---

* This plant is stated by WILLIAMS to be cruciferous, and like the mustard in shape and leaves. See the drawing in the *Pên-ts'ao*, which says it is used as a light aperient.

of ointment of lead on the tips of the flowers. It is as if they told me that the spring is advancing, but the snow is not yet melted. I see a thousand Poppy heads full of black seeds. The east wind will blow and they will be like millet of the best size and quality." The comparison with snow indicates the colour of the Poppies.

YANG SHIH-YING (楊士瀛), a native of Fuhkien when the SUNG dynasty was closing, says in a medical work, while speaking of the use of the Poppy capsule in medicine, in cases of dysentery, "This is thought little of by most, but when dysentery is of long continuance, without gatherings of matter locally and pain resulting, and it is right to use astringents, if this remedy were not at hand how could use be made of this mode of treatment? But there ought to be other drugs accompanying it, to modify the effect."

Use of capsules in dysentery shown by extracts from three authors.

Another SUNG dynasty writer on medicine, named WANG CH'IU (王瑈), in a work to which he gave the name Pai-i-hsüan-fang (百一選方), writes that Poppy seeds and capsules may with advantage be used together for both kinds of dysentery. The seeds are prepared in a pan over the fire. The capsules are roasted on a gridiron. After being pulverised they are made up into pills, with honey, of the size of wu-tung seeds (Eleococca verrucosa). 30 pills are taken at a time, with rice gruel. These pills have been tried and found most efficient.

Another SUNG dynasty author, WANG SHIH (王碩), in his work I-chien-fang (易簡方), says, "The effect of the Poppy capsule in curing dysentery is nothing less than magical. But in its nature it is extremely astringent, and easily causes vomiting and difficulty in digesting food; consequently, patients are afraid of it and do not venture to take it. Yet if it be prepared over the fire with a little vinegar, and black plums be added on account of their acid qualities, its use will be found satisfactory.

"If the four drugs known as the four noble medicines, viz., tang-shên (a coarse ginseng grown in China), pai-shu (Atractylodes alba, a medicinal plant like an artichoke), China-root, and liquorice, be mixed in due proportion and taken with it, there will be still less tendency to check digestion and prevent the food from proceeding on its way. The results will be most excellent."

8°.

LI SHIH-CHÉN (李 時 珍), in the *Pên-ts'ao-kang-mu* (本 草 綱 目), or Chinese *Materia Medica*, follows a chronological order in his arrangement of passages taken from the works of the medical authors who preceded him. It may be concluded, therefore, that the use of the Poppy capsule in medicine began with the SOUTHERN SUNG dynasty, that is, in the latter part of the twelfth or in the thirteenth century. YANG SHIH-YING published his work A.D. 1265, and WANG SIIH is by LI SHIH-CHÉN placed later. The latter does not say whence the use of the capsule was derived; it may therefore be supposed that it was introduced from the West, where its healing virtues were known from the most ancient times.

9°.

In the work called *Hsüan-ming-fang* (宜 明 方), by LIU HO-CHIEN (劉 河 間), of the CHIN (金) dynasty, it is said that for asthmatic cough, with perspiration, in summer and winter of several years' standing, the Poppy capsule may be used. 2½ ounces in weight should be taken. The stem and outer membrane should be removed. Let it simmer in vinegar. Take 1 ounce and mix with half an ounce of black plums; let it be slowly heated and then pulverised. Take for a dose two-tenths of an ounce. Let it be administered in hot water and drunk at bed-time.

LI KAO (李 杲), a physician of the same period (born A.D. 1180, died 1252), says the Poppy capsule is efficient as an astringent and in strengthening the system. It operates on the kidneys, and is useful in the cure of disease affecting the bones.

10°.

WEI I-LIN (危 亦 林), of the YÜAN dynasty, a native of Kiangsi and of the city of Chien-chang, published a book called *Tê-hsiao-fang* (得 效 方), made up of prescriptions collected by himself and his ancestors for four generations before his time. He says that in cases of obstinate diarrhœa of a chronic nature the Poppy capsule may be used. The stringy parts should be removed, and it should be dipped in honey and held over the fire. Then pulverise it. As a dose use half an ounce. Take it with honey and hot water. These capsules have the power to strengthen the constitution. The effect is immediate.

In the YÜAN dynasty the next name is that of CHU CHÊN-HÊNG (朱 震 亨).[*] He says that "The Poppy capsule is used extensively for cough at the present time in the case of those who are weak and consumptive. It is employed to take away the cough. It is used also for diarrhœa and dysentery accompanied with local inflammation. Though its effects are quick, great care must be taken in using it, because it kills like a knife." He also says, "Many persons to cure cough employ the Poppy capsule, and it may be used without fear, but in the first place the root of the disease must be removed, while this should be reserved as a restorative method to complete the cure. In treating dysentery the same is true. Unnatural symptoms have to be expelled and lumps removed. It would not be right to employ at once such medicines as the capsule and *lung-ku* (dragon's bones, certain fossil bones of existing and of extinct animals) in order to check abruptly the action of the stomach and intestines, for the unnatural state of things would reappear with increased severity. Other modifications of an unhealthy kind would supervene, and disease would spread without limit." The expression "it kills like a knife" may be taken as proof that the capsule of which the author is speaking is that of the Opium Poppy.

That a red tint was common in the Poppies of that time may be concluded from the following couplet in a poem of FÊNG TZÛ-CHÊN (馮 子 振), in the YÜAN dynasty:—"They carry in their hair Poppies which are in colour like the red clouds after rain and asters resembling the hoar frost."

11'.

The first name that we meet with in the MING dynasty is that of a brother of the Emperor CH'ÊNG TSU (YUNG LO). He was called CHOU-TING WANG (周 定 王). He says in the *P'u-chi-fang* (普 濟 方) section of *Chiu-huang-pên-ts'ao* (救 荒 本 草), a medical work, "The Poppy capsule prepared in vinegar is to be

The capsule "kills like a knife."

Use of capsules in fourteenth century.

* See for particulars BRETSCHNEIDER's *Botanicon Sinicum*, page 49. He lived in the second half of the fourteenth century. His biography is found in the *Yüan-shih* (元 史).

used for dysentery and bloody evacuations. 1 ounce with half an ounce of orange peel *(ch'ên-p'i)* should be reduced to powder.   For a dose take three-tenths of an ounce with black prunes and hot water."

In the MING dynasty, which lasted through the fifteenth, sixteenth, and part of the seventeenth centuries, the trade of China by sea with India, Arabia, and the islands of the Eastern Archipelago greatly increased ; at that time the Chinese ships, being provided with the mariner's compass,* ventured a little further from land than before, and the extension of the Mongol Empire to Persia had helped to spread intercourse by sea between China and that country.   CHÊNG Ho (鄭和), who was sent on a diplomatic mission to all important seaports from Canton to Aden, succeeded so well on his first voyage that he was repeatedly despatched afterwards, and brought back a fairly minute account of the places he visited.   He was in diplomatic communication with the chief persons in authority in Aden and some other Arabian ports, in Hormuz on the Persian Gulf, in several cities of India, such as Goa, Cochin, Quilon, and Calicut, as well as other centres of trade nearer home. Can we wonder that all the principal exports in those countries became known to the merchants of Canton and Amoy ?   They were then probably, next to the Arabs, the chief traders in the Indian seas.   When the Portuguese appeared unexpectedly at Cochin in 1498, they commenced at once a career of conquest, and quickly made themselves masters of Aden, Hormuz, Goa, Cochin, Calicut, Malacca, and many other cities.   With military prestige they joined great activity in commerce, and became the chief merchants in the East.   At this time, as we learn from BARBOSA, Opium was among the articles brought to Malacca by Arabs and Gentile merchants, to exchange for the cargoes of Chinese junks.   He also states that Opium was taken from Arabia to Calicut, and from Cambay to the same place, the Arabian being one-third higher in price than the Cambay.   The Opium exported from this seaport may be assumed to have been manufactured in Malwa, which lies quite near it.

The Arabs, then, had already begun to grow Opium in India in the sixteenth century.   In addition to this, we are also told that from places on the Coromandel

---

* The floating compass is mentioned by HSÜ CHING (徐兢), ambassador to Corea, as having been in use on board of his ship in his voyage from Ningpo to Corea in the year A.D. 1122.

coast Opium was exported to Siam and Pegu. Here we also find clear indications of the activity of Arab traders in extending the cultivation of the Poppy in India. The Chinese also at this time imported Opium themselves, to be used medically. It is important to note this for the proper understanding of the history of Opium in China.

12°.

WANG HSI (王 璽), an author who died in A.D. 1488, published a work which he named *I-lin-chi-yao* (醫 林 集 要). In it he says that "Opium is produced in Arabia from a Poppy with a red flower. Water should not be allowed. to go over its head. After the flower has faded in the 7th or 8th month the capsule, while still fresh, is pricked for the juice." *First mention of Opium extract was in fifteenth century. Arabian method of obtaining Opium.*

He also says, "In chronic dysentery use Opium of the size of a small bean, and administer it with warm water before the patient takes food (as in the early morning), when the stomach is free. Take one dose a day, and avoid onions, garlic, and soups of all kinds. If thirsty drink water with honey in it." *WANG HSI's directions for use of Opium.*

He also says, "Opium may be used to cure obstinate dysentery of long continuance. When the flower of the Poppy has fallen and the head is developed, after waiting four or five days take a large pricking instrument and prick from 10 to 20 holes in the fresh capsule. Next day, in the morning, when the sap exudes, use a bamboo knife for the purpose of scraping it into an earthenware vessel. Let it dry in a shady place. On each occasion of using it take a piece of the size of a small bean, and let it be administered on an empty stomach and mixed with warm water. Let the patient avoid onions, garlic, and all soups. If he be hot and thirsty let him drink water with honey in it." *WANG HSI's directions for procuring Opium from the Poppy.*

This author, it will be observed, died 10 years before VASCO DE GAMA arrived in India. His biography, in the *History of the Ming Dynasty*, shows that he was in official charge of the province of Kansuh for more than 20 years. His duties included the care of the Mahommedan population of Hami, Turfan, and other western cities. He must have known well the productions, the medical practice, and the customs of the Mahommedan countries; hence his minute acquaintance with Opium. *WANG HSI's knowledge, how acquired.*

Fullest details,
where found.
In the first of the three preceding paragraphs the *Pên-ts'ao* account of WANG's remedy against diarrhœa has been followed ; in the paragraph which comes after it the fuller statement found in the Corean work *Tung-i-pao-chien* (東 醫 寳 鑑) has been given. It seemed better to insert both in this list of passages, because they bear on the point of the manufacture of Opium by the Chinese in their own country in the fifteenth century, of which there can remain little doubt if the extract from the *Tung-i-pao-chien* be fairly considered. The author first mentions the disease and then details the mode in which the medicine which is to cure it may be obtained.

Both accounts are professedly taken from WANG HSI's book. In the absence of the book itself it cannot be decided which is the more correct. Probability is in favour of the last, because it is fuller than the other.

13°.

Mode of preparing
Opium in the
sixteenth century.
In the MING dynasty, in the middle of the sixteenth century, we find an author, LI T'ING (李 挺),* in his work *I-hsiao-ju-mén* (醫 學 入 門), saying Opium or *a-fu-yung* (阿 芙 蓉) is made in the following manner :—Before the head opens the Poppy is approached with a bamboo needle and the capsule pierced in 10 or 15 places, from which sap comes out. The next morning a bamboo knife is used to scrape the sap into a vessel of earthenware. When a good quantity has been collected it is sealed up with paper and placed in the sun for a fortnight, and then the Opium is ready. Its influence and effects are most powerful, and much must not be used.

Medical use.
He also says, " In cases of dysentery with weakness, and when chronic, with all sorts of dysentery indeed, a good remedy will be found in 4 ounces of *huang-lien (Justicia)* prepared over the fire with *wu-chu-yü (Boymia Rutæcarpa)* which has been separately made to simmer in water beforehand. To these are to be added 1 ounce of putchuck and 1 mace of Opium. This mixture is pulverised and rolled into pills with paste made of ground rice. The pills are to be of the size of green beans. 20 or 30 are to be taken at a time, accompanied by a warm

---

* He belonged to Chien-an-fu, in Shensi. There was in the SUNG dynasty another LI T'ING, who wrote on divination and the *I-ching* (易 經).

draught made with the kernels of lotus seeds which have been stewed in water. The patient is then to go to sleep well covered. The effect is marvellous." (Taken from the *Tung-i-pao-chien.*)

This author lived during the time when Foreign trade was prohibited. He ~~Prohibition of Foreign trade encouraged Native production.~~ is mentioned in the *History of the Ming Dynasty* as belonging to the CHIA CHING period (1522 to 1567), after which by a new law European vessels were allowed to trade with China. During the first half of that reign the Japanese made frequent raids upon the Chinese coast. This caused deep indignation, and not only they but all Foreigners were forbidden to trade with China. This was in the year 1523. This naturally rendered Foreign medicines scarce and dear, and therefore we are not surprised to find exact directions given by contemporary medical authors as to how Opium might be manufactured from the Poppy, it being then a highly esteemed drug and having been recommended by medical authors for half a century or more.

14*.

The next author to be cited in the MING dynasty is KUNG YÜN-LIN (龔 雲 林) ~~Kung Yün-lin's prescription.~~ or KUNG HSIN (龔 信). He says in curing white and red dysentery use Opium; putchuck, *huang-lien (Justicia)*, and *pai-shu (Atractylodes)*, each in equal quantity. Pulverise in a mortar and mix into pills with rice, making the pills of the size of a small bean. The old and the young must take half as much as the middle-aged and the strong. Take the mixture with rice water after being without food for some hours. Avoid sour things. Take nothing raw or cold. Take no oil, fat, tea, wine, or flour. The disease will be certainly checked. If thirsty drink a little rice water.

Another method is to take from the bud of the Poppy flower before it has ~~Medical use of Poppy bracts of red and white varieties of Papaver somniferum.~~ opened the two green leaves which enclose it and drop off when the flower opens. Pulverise them and take one-tenth of an ounce with rice water. The effect will be marvellous. According as the diarrhœa is of the red or white kind, use the bracts of the red or white Poppy.

This use of the bracts which envelop the Poppy flower is peculiar to this author. He was a native of Kiangsi and belonged to the Medical Board in Peking.

3

Golden elixir pill. He also made a pill celebrated for its healing power and called the golden elixir. It was thought to be able to cure 24 different diseases, which are detailed in the *Pén-ts'ao* of LI SHIH-CHÉN, with a statement of the decoction to be taken with the pill in each case. In this pill, *I-li-chin-tan* (一 粒 金 丹),* Opium was used to the extent of one-hundredth of an ounce and mixed with glutinous rice, to be divided into three pills, one being a dose. If ineffectual, another was taken. It was forbidden to take many of these pills. Vinegar was not to be used, for fear of internal rupture of the visceral organs resulting in death.

In KUNG SIN'S work, called *Wan-ping-hui-ch'un* (萬 病 回 春), cited in the *Tung-i-pao-chien*, there is another golden elixir, for pain above or below the diaphragm. 2½ mace of Opium, with 1 mace of asafœtida, half a mace of putchuck and of aloes, and a quarter of a mace of cow bezoar. The three last were first pulverised together. Opium and asafœtida were placed in a cup and made liquid by dropping water upon them and stirring over a fire. The whole was mixed with honey and made into pills of the size of green beans, and gilt. When the body was hot the pills were taken with cold water ; when the body was chilled they were taken with boiling water.

The same physician also made purple gold pills with bezoar and other drugs, to help the good effects of Opium. The preceding passages are from LI SHIH-CHÉN and the *Tung-i-pao-chien*.

15°.

Native account of Foreign trade before the prohibition. In the work *Tung-hsi-yang-k'ao* (東 西 洋 考), an account of countries belonging to the Eastern and Western Seas, it is said " In the SUNG dynasty when merchant vessels went to sea the high officials of the ports from which they sailed went to the seashore to escort them. I have gone up the mountain at the entrance of the bight leading to Ch'üan-chou-fu (Amoy) and seen the inscriptions, with dates, on the rocks which record these things. At that time the regulations were very stringent, as if the matters in hand were of great importance. In the province of Fuhkien, in

---

* This was also used in Peking, says LI SHIH-CHÉN, as an aphrodisiac and quite extensively, beyond the range of regular medicine.

the SUNG and YÜAN dynasties, Superintendents of Foreign Trade were appointed at each port, under the name *Shih-po-ssŭ* (市 舶 司). At the beginning of the present dynasty (MING) this system remained unaltered, but was afterwards allowed to fall into neglect. In the period from 1465 to 1506 it happened that in the more powerful families connected with commerce there were adventurous persons who went on large ships beyond seas to trade. There were at that time bad men who secretly opened out new paths in which to gain profit, while the officers placed in charge failed to secure, openly at least, in these profitable transactions any share for the Government. At first they succeeded in gradually enriching themselves, but in course of time this sort of trade degenerated into a rivalry as to who should shoot his arrow farthest and into various irregular proceedings." The same work further says that "Along the seashore there is much land which is so full of potash and soda that the farmer can realise no harvests from it. It is only possible to look on the sea as the soil to be worked. This led to various employments connected with the sea. The rich collected a revenue from imported goods, and safely brought back with them the sheaves which they reaped in the harvest of the waters. The poor also laboured for a wage, and stretched out the hand to seize the pint measure of rice which they needed to support them in their toil. But the day of rigorous prohibition [Bad effects of prohibition.] arrived. These people could not, as before, gain a living through the arrival of merchant ships. They were strong and hearty. They would not fold their hands and sit down inactive in poverty and want. Troubles consequently occurred in succession, resulting in disturbances of the public peace. Men of this class hid themselves in places beyond the local jurisdiction, and having rudely impinged on the law's net they dared not return to be apprehended. In addition to this they conducted barbarians from a distance on various occasions into the places to which they belonged."

The author proceeds to say that when the prohibition was withdrawn from [Good effects of permission to trade.] Foreign commerce and revenue collected from goods and merchant vessels, the Government gained in revenue and the people in tranquillity. In particular the local military expenditure was supplied to a fixed extent each year from this source. He then remarks, "The duties levied were of three kinds, according to the rules then in force : [Duties levied.]

there was the water duty, the land duty, and the supplementary duty. The water duty was tonnage, and was levied on the representative of the ship. The land duty was duty on goods, fixed *ad valorem*, and levied, according to the quantity of goods, on the merchant doing business on shore. In respect to this, from fear of smuggling, it was the rule that the supercargo *(ch'uan-shang)* should not deliver goods until the presentation of a memorandum addressed to the merchant on shore who was the buyer of goods, stating the amount of duty for the goods mentioned, and directing him to go to the vessel and pay the duties there; after this the goods might be removed. As to the supplementary duties, they were levied in case of an error in the declared measurement of the vessel in feet, to be added to (or subtracted from) the tonnage."

Tariff of A.D. 1589. Further, in the year 1589 a tariff was issued, stating the duties to be levied on each kind of goods and approved by the military commandant. In this tariff myrrh, gum olibanum, and asafœtida, with other articles, are entered at a fixed rate of $3\frac{1}{2}$ mace per cwt. for myrrh, and 2 mace per cwt. for the other two. Opium is Tariff of A.D. 1615. rated at 2 mace of silver for 10 catties, or 2 ounces per cwt. In the year 1615 a new tariff was issued, in which Opium appears rated at $1\frac{73}{100}$ mace for each 10 catties.

16°.

Li Shih-chên's Materia Medica. Li Shih-chên, author of the *Pên-ts'ao-kang-mu*, finished that work A.D. 1578. After saying that the Poppy is called *yü-mi* (御 米) because it is a grain *(mi)* which can be used in making presents, and *hsiang-ku* (象 穀) because it resembles millet *(ku)*, he adds that it is sown in autumn, and in winter is above ground in the form of tender stalks which may be used as food and constitute an excellent vegetable, the leaves being like lettuce. In the 3rd or 4th month the flowering part of the plant is well advanced and protected by bracts, which fall off when the flower opens. There are four petals, which, taken together, are as large as a saucer. The capsule is in the centre of the flower, folded in stamens. The flower falls on the third day after opening, leaving the capsule at the top of the stem. It is 1 or 2 inches in length, and in size like the *ma-tou-ling* (a drug, capsule of the bladder tree). It has a lid and a short stalk. In shape it is much like a wine jar. In it there are many white grains, which can be used for making a sort of porridge for taking with ordinary food. If the seeds are ground with water, and mixed with green beans first ground so as to make a jelly, it will be found excellent. Oil also can be made from the seeds. As to the capsules, they are much used in medicine, but are not mentioned in the old *Pharmacopœia*. From this it may be concluded that in ancient times the capsules were not used.

The author refers here to the NORTHERN SUNG dynasty, A.D. 960 to 1126, when the Poppy first appeared in the *Pharmacopœia*.

He proceeds, "In Kiangsu the double Poppy is called *li-ch'un-hua* (麗 春 花), flower of the bright spring. This is said by some to be a variety of the *ying-su-hua* (罌 粟 花); but this is a mistake. Its flower changes perpetually. It may be white, or red, purple, pink, or apricot yellow, or it may be half red or half purple and half white, and is very beautiful, and this is the reason that it is called the *li-ch'un*. It is also known as the Moutan pæony's rival and the flower of the embroidered coverlid." He also says of the seeds of the Poppy that they cure diarrhœa and relieve feverish symptoms, and of the capsules that for medicinal purposes they should be well washed and softened in water. "The stalk and outer skin should be removed and also the stringy fibres within. Let them be dried in a dark place and cut very small. They are then to be well mixed with rice vinegar and placed over the fire to simmer, after which they are fit for use as a drug. They may also be prepared with honey instead of vinegar. In taste and nature the capsules thus prepared are sour, astringent, and slightly cooling, without being poisonous. With vinegar, black prunes, or orange peel they are most effectual in curing diarrhœa, asthma, rheumatism, or pain in the heart and abdomen."

Proceeding to speak of Opium, he says, "Formerly Opium was not much heard of; recently it has been used by some in medical recipes. It is said to be the juice of the *ying-su-hua* (or Poppy). While the head of this flower is still green, in the afternoon take a large needle and prick the outside skin, taking care not to wound the inner hard shell. It is to be pricked in from three to five places. The next day, when the sap has come out, take a bamboo knife and scrape it into an earthenware cup. Let it be dried in the shade. It being made in this way accounts for the fact that this article when bought in shops has mixed with it pieces of the skin of the capsule. It is a sour astringent, and can cure, etc. Especially is the elixir *I-li-chin-tan*, made with it, useful for curing a hundred diseases."

17°.

In the *Tu-shu-chi-ch'êng* we find a passage from a work on flowers by an author named WANG SHIH-MOU (王 世 懋), who lived at the end of the sixteenth century.* He says, "After the pæony *(shao-yao)* the Poppy is the most beautiful of flowers, and grows most luxuriantly. It changes readily. If care be taken in watering and planting, it becomes very handsome, and assumes a thousand varieties of shape and colour. It even becomes yellow or green. Looked at from a distance it is lovely; when nearer it becomes less attractive. I have heard that the seeds can be used as food, and have a strongly astringent effect."

In the work on flowers published in the time of KANG HSI, under the name *Kuang-ch'ün-fang-p'u*, there is a poem on the Poppy by WU YU-P'EI (吳 幼 培), of the MING dynasty. "In the court which fronts the hall, a long way down, when the daylight is lengthened, before the terrace are flowers of the genii breathing out abundant fragrance. A vapour encircles them, and there are rain drops upon them, where they put forth their lovely forms. They have a red tint and glossy lustre, and their appearance is beautiful. They are sown in mid-autumn and must wait for the coming year. They open their flowers in early summer and are companions to the declining sun. Another thing to be praised is their seeds, heaped up in large capsules one after the other. Why, then, be content with what is ugly and only gather rice and such-like grain ?"

In the *Tu-shu-chi-ch'êng* there is a passage from a work called *Ts'ao-hua-p'u* (草 花 譜), the book of plants and flowers, which says, "The Poppy has a thousand petals and all the five colours. Its petals are shorter than those of the flower called *yü-mei-jên*, and more graceful. Through the whole garden the spring alighting upon them they seem to fly as they move to the breeze. The seeds are sown in spring,"

* He died 1590. *See* Biography 175 in *Ming History.*

18*.

In the work called *Wu-li-hsiao-shih* (物 理 小 識), written at the end of the Míng dynasty and the beginning of the present, it is said of the Poppy that it is sown in the middle month of autumn, at noon. After flowering, the seed vessel grows into the shape of a vase. The tiny seeds can be eaten as porridge. Oil is also obtained from them, and the capsules are useful in medicine; they are powerfully astringent. When the capsules are still green, if a needle be used to puncture them in 10 or 15 places, the sap will come out. This should be received into an earthenware cup, which may be covered carefully with paper pasted round the edge. Let the cup be exposed to the sun for 14 days; it is then Opium, ready for use as an astringent, and restrains reproduction most powerfully.

Another account of the mode of obtaining Opium from the Poppy.

19*.

Carefully weighing what is said in the passages preceding, it appears plain that from the latter part of the fifteenth century the manufacture of Native Opium has existed in China, and it is not only in recent years that there has been both Native and Foreign Opium in this country. Let the reader examine the various accounts of the manipulation by four different authors. WANG HSI's book cannot now be procured, but judging by what is quoted from him in LI SHIH-CHÊN's work, he meant to describe the method of Poppy culture in Arabia, and spoke particularly of a kind which yielded the Opium sap in the 7th and 8th months or later. When, however, he speaks, as in the passage translated from the *Tung-i-pao-chien*, of obstinate diarrhœa needing Opium to cure it, and advises the physician to make Opium direct from the Poppy in a way which he describes, he must be speaking of a Chinese made article. LI T'ING's account differs in too many points from that of WANG HSI to be regarded as a second-hand statement based exclusively upon it. If so, then LI T'ING is a third and independent witness on this subject, the fourth being the author of the work *Wu-li-hsiao-shih*.

Résumé.

20°.

Early in the seventeenth century a Dutch physician named JACOBUS BONTIUS went to reside at Batavia, and died there. What he wrote on medicine was afterwards included in the work of GULIELMUS PISO, *De Indiæ utriusque Re naturali et medica Libri XIV* (ELZEVIR, 1658).* The preface of BONTIUS is dated Batavia, 1629. He says that those nations which use Opium seem drowsy, and are dull in commerce and in arms; but unless we had Opium to use in these hot countries, in cases of dysentery, cholera, burning fever, and various bilious affections, we should practise medicine in vain. This was the basis of the ancient medicines, theriac, mithridate, and philonium.

The poor Indians use the leaves and branches of the Poppy to prepare an inferior sort of Opium, which they obtain by drying in the sun. This they call *pust*, and they themselves are nicknamed *pusti*. The rich, who indulge in the more expensive drug, are known as *afyáni*. The Greeks knew the danger of Opium but not its merits, which are clearly divine, and which they failed sufficiently to explore.

BONTIUS prescribed curcuma, made from Opium and the Indian crocus, *Hsi-tsang-hung-hua* (西藏紅花). This was his refuge in dysentery, cholera, phrenitis, and spasms. He took refuge in Opium as a sacred anchor, he tells us, in desperate cases. He used Poppy seeds and Poppy heads. He says that Opium helps nature to conquer the enemy by inducing sleep, and that he could prepare it so that it should not injure even an infant.

21°.

Towards the end of the MING dynasty the practice of taking Opium medically or otherwise by swallowing it was destined to be soon changed for the habit of Opium-smoking. It is requisite, therefore, in proceeding with this record to enter on the subject of tobacco and tobacco-smoking, in order to introduce by easy transition this new step taken by the Chinese in the use of Opium.

* Kindly lent by Dr. E. BRETSCHNEIDER.

22°.

In the latter years of the MING dynasty tobacco cultivation and tobacco-smoking were introduced into China from the Philippine Islands. Here the Spaniards had settled, and they were in constant communication with America. The tobacco plant crossed the Pacific and flourished in the neighbourhood of Manila. The first place in China where it was planted was at Amoy; it was brought there by Fuhkien sailors trading to Manila. In the work above cited under the name *Wu-li-hsiao-shih*, written about A.D. 1650, we are told that tobacco was brought to China about A.D. 1620, which would be about the same time that King JAMES I's *Counterblast to Tobacco* was being circulated in England as a new publication. Tobacco was called the "smoke plant" or *tampaku*, or *tan-pu-kuei* (淡 不 鬼).

In the time of the last MING Emperor, who reigned from 1628 to 1644, tobacco-smoking was prohibited, but the habit spread too rapidly to be checked by law. The origin of Opium-smoking is thus accounted for. Various ingredients were in various countries mixed with tobacco to try their effect; among them was Opium. Arsenic was another ingredient, which is still used by the Chinese in what is called "water tobacco."

The Manchus now took the place of the MING dynasty. There is a historical work called the *Tung-hua-lu* (東 華 錄), which gives the events of the first century of Manchu rule in the form of a chronicle. In the year 1641 there is in this book an account of an edict which has reference to tobacco. The Emperor asks the princes and high officers, "Why do you not lead the soldiers yourselves in the practice of archery? The elder youths should practise the horn-bow and winged arrow; the younger should be skilled in using the wooden bow and willow-twig arrow. Our dynasty in military exercises makes archery the chief thing. To smoke tobacco is a fault, but not so great a fault as to neglect bow exercise. As to the prohibition of tobacco-smoking, it became impossible to maintain it, because you princes and others smoked privately, though not publicly; but as to the use of the bow, this must not be neglected." The edicts afterwards promulgated against Opium were just as

Tobacco-smoking, when introduced.

Prohibition of tobacco-smoking.

Manchu prohibition of tobacco-smoking.

4

ineffectual as those against tobacco-smoking; and among the causes of their failure must be included the love of Opium-smoking by many in high positions, favourites and others, whom it would be very difficult to punish.

Spread of
tobacco-smoking.
In a work called *Shun-hsiang-chui-pi* (幕 鄉 賢 筆), written 10 or 20 years later than this edict, tobacco-smoking is described as spreading to the city of Soochow and as being quickly adopted by all classes of the people. The author states that this circumstance was much to the detriment of morality; it had previously been a difficult thing to uphold moderation in living, but after this it was far more so. Women as well as men, the inhabitants of villages as well as of large towns, fell into the snare, till the habit became almost universal. This immense popularity of tobacco-smoking was an indication of the readiness of the Chinese nation to adopt the use of narcotics. The same thing which took place in the nineteenth century with Opium-smoking occurred in the seventeenth century with tobacco-smoking. The Confucian mind was shocked, the sense of propriety was wounded; but this did not prevent the rapid spread of both these modes of indulgence in all circles. Prohibitory edicts were issued in vain by Emperors animated by paternal affection for their people. Tobacco was a less evil than they supposed; Opium-smoking was a far greater evil than they feared. In both cases the Emperor was powerless. The Emperor CH'ÊNG TSUNG, as we ought to call him, but who is better known as TAO KUANG, is much to be respected for his strong moral convictions on the subject of Opium. He made really great efforts to cope with this evil, but it was in vain. The fondness of the people for inhaling a narcotic was too strong for him to overcome. He failed utterly in the attempt to put down Opium-smoking even in the city of Peking. It was as hard to persuade his own people to abandon a bad habit as to conquer England in war.

Opium-smoking
in Formosa.
The habit of tobacco-smoking became national, and went on extending itself for a century, till soon after the close of the long reign of KANG HSI the attention of the Government was drawn to Opium-smoking as a new vice in Formosa and at Amoy. It grew up in the same part of the country where tobacco-smoking had been introduced.

23°.

One of the most valuable works to be consulted on the subject of early Opium- Kæmpfer's Amœnitates exoticæ.
smoking, its connexion with tobacco-smoking, and the Opium trade as it existed at
the end of the seventeenth century, is the *Amœnitates exoticæ* of KÆMPFER. Some
passages from this work, recording his observations on tobacco, hemp, and Opium,
will now be given. They were first published in 1712, but the original notes from
which they were compiled were taken 20 years earlier.

" Nicotiana ante sesqui circiter secula toti antiquo orbi, adeoque et Persiæ, Tobacco: Kæmpfer's account.
cœpit a Lusitanis transvectoribus innotescere.   Nomen ubique habet *tabaci*, et
pro diverso gentium idiomate *tobak, tabacco, tombak* et *tembakú*, ab insula hujus
nominis Americana, quæ herbæ copiam inventoribus dederat.   Plantæ vix nomen
innotuerat, quin simul cultura celebrari ubique cœperit, et fumandi usus omne
humanum genus stupenda velocitate incantaverit.   Plantam, Hyosciami speciem si
negamus, ex classe tamen venenatarum nequaquam eximenda fuerit; cum vertigines,
anxietates et vomitus, quos fumigata in non adsuetis concitat, malignitatis testes
sint luculenti.   Experimentis Redianis constat, olei ejus guttulam recenti immissam
vulneri, pullos volucrium enecare, hominibus vero inferre periculosa symptomata.
Vidi bajulos circa Casanam Tartariæ, qui perforatum cornu bubulum foliis plenum,
superpositis carbonibus, paucis haustibus evacuabant; ex quo instar epilepticorum
prosternebantur, pituita spumoque diffluentes.   Quam vero venenata sint folia,
eorum tamen fumus consuetudine homini fit familiaris, ut, non modo non noceat
malignitate sua, sed benigniori sale serum ex capitis recessibus eliciat, ac cerebrum
hilaritate impleat.   Quod ut præstet felicius, Persæ fumum trahunt per machinam,
aqua ultra dimidium plenam, quæ fœtidum et cerebro inimicum sulphur imbibens,
fumum transmittit ab omni malignitatis acrimonia defæcatum, frigefactum et
sincerum.   Machina illa, quam كاليان *khaliaan* vel *khaliuun* vocant, ampulla est
sesquipedalis altitudinis, vitrea, oblongo donata collo; cujus orificium claudit orbiculus
æneus, in sesquipalmarem diametrum expansus, duos in medio permittens tubulos
invicem adsolidatos, æneos; unum, cujus inferior pars in ampullam demissa, aquæ
immergitur; superior recipit nicotianæ cum impositis carbonibus retinaculum, in-

fundibulo seu buccinæ orificio simile : alterum breviorem, cujus demissa extremitas

[Pipe for smoking tobacco through water.]

aquam non attingit : superior incurvata arundinem excipit longam, qua fumus
attrahitur. Tubulorum propago, proxime sub orbiculo, tela xylina arcte circumvoluta
est, in eam crassitiem, quæ vitri orificium cum modica colli parte explent atque
claudat arctissime : ita evenit, ut ad suctum non possit nisi ex infundibulo fumus
succedere ; qui jucundo strepitu aquam penetrans, primo inane vitri spatium occupat,
inde per arundinem ad os sugentis atque ipsos pulmones pertingit ; attractio enim,
non bucca aut labiis, ut vulgo solet, sed toto pectore peragitur, quo ipso fumus
per pulmones se diffundit. Si acrior herba sit, concisam prius aquæ immergunt
exprimuntque, ut a crudiori acrimonia liberetur : quod idem a Sinensibus et
Japonibus factitatum vidi. Modum fumandi per machinam a Persis edocti sunt
Arabes Hindostani, seu Indi magni Mogolis, et, qui cum religione mores Arabum
adoptarunt, nigritæ quidam insulares ; sed his, quod vitra deficiant, pro ampulla
servit excavatus cortex cucurbitarum. Turci, Sinenses, Japones, Europæorum more
fumum trahunt per fistulam, receptaculo tabaci accensi insertam. Nigritæ gentiles
fumum sine instrumento hauriunt, rotatis foliis in turbinem, cujus basin accendunt,
apice labris retento et sucto."

The Persian pipe for smoking tobacco through water here described by the Hookah or water pipe. traveller is the parent of that now in use among the Chinese, and of the Indian hookah. The Persians taught its use to the Arabs of Hindustan, the Hindus, and the black inhabitants of Asiatic islands. It spread with the religion of the Arabs wherever they went.

According to KÆMPFER's account, tobacco-smoking had during a century and Summary of KÆMPFER's account. a half been gradually spreading through all countries. It was introduced into Persia by the Portuguese while prosecuting their trading operations in the ports of the Persian Gulf. The poisonous qualities of tobacco he proves by what he had himself seen of its effects. Fowls die if tobacco oil is injected into a recent wound. He saw at Kasan porters smoking in a peculiar way. They filled a cow's horn with tobacco leaves, placed it over burning coals, and smoked through a hole in the horn; after a few whiffs they fell down in a state of something like foaming epilepsy. Yet, he adds, when smokers are accustomed to the use of tobacco it soothes the brain and promotes cheerfulness.

The invention of the water pipe was intended to assist in removing the Object of the water pipe. poisonous and unpleasant qualities of tobacco. The smoke on passing through the water is free from sulphurous fumes, moderated in strength, cooled, and purified. Glass vessels were first used, with brass fittings. The Natives of the Eastern Archipelago, not having glass, used the calabash instead.

The author adds that while the Turks, Chinese, and Japanese all smoke with Cigars. a pipe, like the Europeans, the black Natives of the islands have a way of their own; they roll the tobacco leaves into a twist, which they light at one end and smoke from at the other.

"Alterum atque interni usus *kheif* ex papavere sumitur: quo Indi Persæque How Opium is made in Persia. hortos et agros conserunt, ut lactescentem succum ex læsis capitibus proliciant. Hunc succum Europa *Opium*; Asia cum Ægypto *afiuun* et *ofiuun* vocat. Persia idem præparatum, ex reverentia, appellat *theriaki*, i.e., Theriacam; nam hæc illis est poetarum illa *galene, hilare* et *eudios*, id est, medicina animo serenitatem, hilaritatem et tranquillitatem conferens : quo olim tergemino elogio theriacale antidotum Andromachi appellatum legimus.   In Perside collectio ejus celebratur per ineuntem æstatem, propinqua maturitati capita decussatim sauciando per superficiem.   Culter negotio servit quintuplici acie instructus, qui una sectione quinque infligit vulnera longa parallela.   Ex vulnusculis promanans succus postridie scalpro abstergitur, et in vasculum, abdomini præligatum, colligitur.   Tum altera capitum facies eodem modo vulneratur, ad liquorem pariter proliciendum.   At, hæc collectio, ob capitum impar incrementum et magnitudinem, aliquoties in eodem arvo instituenda est.   Solent in plantis nimium ramosis superflua capita prius amputari : sic reliqua magis grandescunt, et succo implentur majoris efficaciæ.   Primæ collectionis lacryma, *gobaar* dicta, præstantior est, et graviori pollet cerebrum demulcendi virtute, colorem exhibens albidum, vel ex luteo pallentem ; sed qui color ex longiori insolatione et ariditate infuscari solet.   Altera collectio succum promit, priori, ut virtute, ita pretio inferiorem, coloris plerumque obscuri, vel ex rufo nigricantis.   Sunt, qui et tertiam instituunt, qua obtinetur lacryma nigerrima et exiguæ virtutis.

"Præparatio Opii potissimum in eo consistit, ut, aquæ pauxillo humectatum, spatha crassa lignea continuo et fortiter ducatur et reducatur in patina lignea et plana, donec elaboratissimæ picis consistentiam, tenacitatem et nitorem induat.   Ita diu multumque subactum, ad ultimum manu non nihil pertractatur nuda, et demum, in cylindros breves rotatum, venale exponitur ; forcipe dividendum, cum particulas emptores petunt.   Hac serie pertractatum Opium appellatur *theriaak malidèh*, i.e., theriaca molendo præparata, vel etiam *theriaak afiuun*, id est, theriaca opiata, ad differentiam theriacæ Andromachi, quam illi vocant *theriaak farunk.*   Præparandi hic labor perpetuus est propolarum, quos vocant *kheifruus*, quasi Germanice diceres *trunken Krämere*, quo illi, in foris et quadriviis sedentes, brachia sua strenue exercent.   Massa hæc sæpe numero, non aqua, sed melle subigitur, ea copia admisso, quæ non siccitatem modo, sed et amaritiem temperet : et hæc specialiter appellatur *bœhrs.*   Insignior præparatio est, qua inter agitandum adduntur nux myristica, cardamomum, cinamomum et macis, in pulverem subtilissimum redacta ; qualiter præparatum Opium cordi et cerebro insigniter prodesse creditur.   Vocatur in specie *polonià*, vel, ut alii pronunciant, *folonià*, puta *Philonium Persicum*, seu *mesue.*

Alii omissis aromatibus, tantum croco et ambra massam infarciunt. Multi præparationem in usum proprium ipsi perficiunt domi suæ, ne a propolis admiscendorum paucitate vel multitudine decipiantur. Præter hoc triplicis præparationis Opium, quod sola pilularum forma deglutitur, prostat, vel etiam a domesticis conficitur, liquor celebris nominis *cocondr* dictus, Græcorum quod puto **Μηκώνιον** ac Homerianum *nepenthes*, quod a bibacibus propinari affatim per horarum intervalla solet. Parant hujus liquorem alii ex foliis, aqua simplici per brevem moram coquendis ; alii ex capitibus contusis infusione macerandis, vel iisdem supra filtrum repositis, aquam eandem septies octiesve superfundendo : admixtis pro cujusque placito, quæ sapori gratiam concilient. Tertium addo opiati genus, electuarium lætificans et lætificando inebrians ; hujus electuarii, cujus basin idem Opium etiam constituit, a seplasiariis et medicis, prout quisque ingenio pollet, varie elaboratur, ac diversis ingredientibus ad roborandos et exhilarandos spiritus dirigitur; unde variæ ejus extant descriptiones; quarum primaria et famosissima est, quæ debetur inventori HASJKM *Begi*, quandoquidem comedentis animum miris perfundere gaudiis, et magicis cerebrum demulcere ideis et voluptatibus dicitur.

"Opium quod Europæis, si grani unius vel paucorum dosin excesseris, lethiferum nefas audit, a prænominatis populis longa adsuetudine ita familiare redditum est, ut drachmam multi sine noxa deglutiant. Multa hoc abusu, vel longiori ejus usu, acciuntur mala ; emaciatur enim corpus, laxantur vires, contristatur animus, stupescit ingenium : unde videas instar stipitum somnolentos et quasi elingues sedere in conviviis opii liguritores. Sæpe oblati mihi sunt, quos a canino appetitu Opii percurarem, sostro centum aureorum promisso, si hoc citra damnum et vitæ dispendium præstitero. Exempla Opii voracium non est, quod adducam, cum eorum pleni sint medicorum libri. Capita papaveris teneriora aceto condita nonnulli in mensa secunda appetunt ; alii alia ex iisdem sorbilla conficiunt, pro suo quique placito."

KÆMPFER proceeded from Persia in June 1688 to Batavia, which city—then, Kæmpfer's visit to Java in 1688. as now, the chief seat of the Dutch power in the East—he reached in September 1689, after visiting the settlements of that nation in Arabia Felix, India, Ceylon, and the island of Sumatra. He staid in Java eight months, and then went to Japan. Of the use of Opium in Java he gives the following account :—

Mention of use of Opium.

"De Opio, ejusque Persis et Indis communi usu, diximus. Addo abusum execrabilem, qui viget inter Indos nigritas, ad efferandum animos ad homicidiorum patrandorum audaciam ; dum vel vitæ suæ, vel injuriarum pertæsi, se devovent morti, per ultionem et mortes aliorum oppetendæ. Eo fine Opii deglutiunt bolum : ex quo intentionis idea exasperatur, turbatur ratio, et infrænus redditur animus, adeo, ut stricto pugione, instar tigridum rabidarum, excurrant in publicum, obvios quosvis, sive amicos, sive inimicos, trucidaturi, donec ipsi, ab alio perforati, prosternantur. Actus hic vocatur *hamik*, apud incolas Javæ et ulterioris Orientis crebro spectabilis. Vocabuli sonum ibi horret, quicunque audit ; nam qui vident homicidam, illi vocem *hamik* summopere exclamant : monituri inermes, ut fugiant, et vitæ suæ prospiciant : dum ad extinguendam beluam accurrere debet, quisquis armatus et cordatus est. Opii etiam externus usus est apud nigritas : nam eodem aqua diluto nicotianam inficiunt, ut accensa caput vehementius turbet. Vidi in Java tabernas levidenses ex arundine, in quibus id genus tabaci hauriendum exponebatur prætereuntibus. Nulla per Indiam merx majori lucro divenditur a Batavis, quam *afiuun*, quo carere adsueti non possunt, nec potiri, nisi navibus Batavorum ex Bengala et Choromandela advecto.

First Opium-smoking shops.

The *tabernæ levidenses ex arundine* here spoken of were the first Opium-smoking shops of which we have any record. According to the statement here given, Opium diluted with water was smoked with tobacco. This sort of tobacco was exposed to passers-by to be smoked when, two centuries ago, the learned German traveller was taking walks in Batavia to observe the customs of the Native population. He uses the word *haurio;* that this here means smoking, and not drinking, is plain from another passage (in *Amœnitates exoticæ,* page 642), where he says the black inhabitants smoke without a pipe *(sine instrumento hauriunt),* by rolling tobacco leaves into a whirl, which they light at the lower end and smoke from at the upper by holding it with their lips and drawing. Of Opium from the Coromandel coast, which then formed a part of the lading of the Batavian ships to take back to Java, we now hear nothing; but the Bengal portion of this lucrative trade finds its lineal successor in the Patna Opium of the present day.

24°.

In the year 1723, shortly before the first edict against Opium-smoking, a medical work was published with the name *Chi-yen-liang-fang* (急慶真方),* by NIEN HSI-YAO (年 希 堯), a bannerman in Peking of high rank and great influence in his day. He places among his prescriptions a pill called *Wan-ying-tan* (萬應 丹), made of Opium mixed with bezoar, camphor, and other drugs, 13 in all. He states that it could cure the diseases of all seasons, including fevers beginning with chill *(shang-han)*, epidemic fever, heat apoplexy (*chung-shu*, severe or slight), paralysis, headache, slight fever, vomiting with diarrhœa, ague, pain in the heart, abdominal pain, and the like. Two pills are prescribed for severe cases, and one when the attack is slight; they are to be taken with cold water.

He also recommends a plaster called *Yü-chên-kao* (毓 麟 膏), to be attached at the navel. It adds to the vigour of the body and saves it from decay, warms the kidneys, strengthens the loins and knees, removes cold and wet chill, with all abdominal pains, and is useful for healing all sorts of affections to which men and women are subject. It is made by mixing Opium, musk, *yang-ch'i-shih* (陽起石), olibanum, cloves, and the like; 14 other drugs are added. By gradual decoction it is prepared for use and employed as required. There is another prescription, called the *Pao-yang-ling-kuei-shên-fang* (保 養 靈 龜 神 方), or marvellous recipe of the efficacious tortoise for the preservation of health; it is formed by mixing Opium with *ch'an-su* (a medicine made of the oily part of toads) and such things, and adding 33 other kinds of medicine. It is prepared with oil for use.

25°.

There is a work on Formosa called *T'ai-hai-ts'ai-fêng-t'u-k'ao* (臺海採風圖考), which was published in 1746. It contains extracts from earlier works, and among them one by a native of Peking named HUANG YÜ-PU (黃玉圃), who was at some earlier date sent to Formosa and wrote an account of what he saw there, which was published under the name *T'ai-hai-shih-ch'a-lu* (臺海使槎錄). He gives the following statements from this work on the subject of Opium-smoking. Opium for smoking

* Kindly lent by Dr. DUDGEON.

is prepared by mixing hemp and the (root of the) grasscloth plant *(Pachyrizus angulatus* or, may be, *Pueraria Thunbergia*, Dr. BRETSCHNEIDER) with Opium, and cutting them up small. This mixture is boiled with water in a copper pan or tripod. The Opium so prepared is mixed with tobacco. A bamboo tube is also provided, the end of which is filled with coir fibres from the coir palm. Many persons collect this Opium to smoke mixed with tobacco. The price asked is several times greater than for tobacco alone. Those who make it their sole business to prepare Opium in this way are known as Opium tavern keepers. Those who smoke once or twice form a habit which cannot afterwards be broken off. Warmth is conveyed in a vaporous form to the *tan-t'ien* * ("red field," located in the kidneys), so that the whole night can be passed without lying down. The aborigines smoke as an aid to vice. The limbs grow thin and appear to be wasting away; the internal organs collapse. The smoker unless he be killed will not cease smoking. The local officers have from time to time strictly prohibited the habit. It has often been found that when the time came for administering the bastinado to culprits of this class, they would beg for a brief respite, that they might first take another smoke. Opium came from Java.

Opium-smoking came to Formosa from Java.

Of the various early narratives which describe the habit of smoking Opium with a bamboo pipe, the account we have here seems to be the most minute. It is not stated in what year it was written, but the year in which it was reprinted as an extract was 1746. In reference to the last sentence, which says that Opium came from Java, it should be observed that it agrees with what KÆMPFER in his book states. He found that diluted Opium was mixed with tobacco to offer to passers-by to smoke; he observed this during his residence in Java. We learn from this that it was tobacco-smoking which led to Opium-smoking. During the reign of KANG HSI KOXINGA occupied Formosa for a time. It was about that time that the island received the name "Taiwan." In the MING dynasty we meet only with the names Tamsui and Kelung. In the days of KOXINGA many Chinese colonists went over from the mainland to reside there. There was constant communication with Java

---

* The 丹田 is threefold. The seat of the *tsing* (semen) is 3 inches below the navel; that of breath is in the brain. The seat of the soul is in the heart. The first is here chiefly meant. See *Tung-i-pao-chien*, I, 12.

by trading vessels. Many wanderers without a livelihood from various countries
went there from time to time, and it was through this class of persons that the
pernicious habit of Opium-smoking originated in Formosa.

26°.

In the work named *Tai-wan-chih* (台灣志), or topographical account of
Taiwan,* it is said, " It is not known from what place the practice of Opium-smoking
was introduced. The Opium is boiled in a copper pan. The pipe used for smoking is
in appearance like a short club. Depraved young men without any fixed occupation
used to meet together by night to smoke; it grew to be a custom with them.
Often various delicacies prepared with honey and sugar, with fresh fruits, to the
number of 10 or more dishes, were provided for visitors while smoking. In order
to tempt new smokers to come, no charge was made for the first time. After some
time they could not stay away, and would come even if they forfeited all their
property. Smokers were able to remain awake the whole night and rejoiced, as
an aid to sensual indulgence. Afterwards they found themselves beyond the
possibility of cure. If for one day they omitted smoking, their faces suddenly
became shrivelled, their lips opened, their teeth were seen, they lost all vivacity,
and seemed ready to die. Another smoke, however, restored them. After three
years all such persons die. It is said that the barbarian inhabitants of Formosa
thus use craft and cunning in order to cheat the Chinese residents out of their
money at the expense of their lives. The foolish are not sensible of their danger,
and fall victims. This habit has entered China about 10 or more years. There are
many smokers in Amoy, but Formosa is the place where this vice has been most
injurious. It is truly sad to reflect on this."

Another account of early Opium-smoking in Formosa.

27.

In the year A.D. 1729 an edict was issued on Opium-smoking, prohibiting
the sale of Opium and the opening of Opium-smoking houses. The Government

Prohibitory edict of 1729.

* Kindly lent by Dr. DUDGEON, who was the first to discover the Native account of the origin and first
progress of Opium-smoking in Formosa.

found itself face to face with a dangerous social evil of an alarming kind. The physical effects of Opium-smoking as displayed in the shrivelling up of the features and an early death, as thus described by eye-witnesses, produced a deep impression in Peking. The sellers of Opium were to be punished, not the buyers. The masters of Opium shops are dealt with most severely, as being the seducers into evil paths of the young members of respectable families. Sellers of Opium were to bear the wooden collar for a month, and be banished to the frontier. The keepers of shops were to be punished in the same way as propagators of depraved doctrines; that is, they were to be strangled after a few months' imprisonment. Their assistants were to be beaten with 100 blows, and banished 1,000 miles. Everyone was to be punished except the smoker; for example, boatmen, local bailiffs, neighbours lending help, soldiers, police runners, in any way connected with the matter, all had punishments assigned them. The same was true of magistrates and Custom House Superintendents in the sea-port towns where these things had happened; all were to bear some penalty. Only the Opium-smoker was exempted. It was felt, perhaps, that his punishment was self-inflicted; he would die without the help of the law. This edict was followed by another the next year for the checking of evil practices among the colonists of Formosa. All guilty of robbery, false evidence, enticing the aborigines to commit murder, the sale of gambling instruments or of Opium for smoking, are to be punished with death or banishment.

Spread of Opium-smoking in the eighteenth century. Opium-selling for smoking purposes has from this time forward been regarded as a crime by the ruling authorities. From their point of view it is considered as criminal in proportion to the mischief it causes, which is without doubt great beyond computation. The very earliest instance of legislation on this matter is here before the reader. It was based on local events occurring on the sea-coast, a long way from Peking. The gradual spread from the province of Fuhkien to all the provinces was still in the future and was not before the minds of the legislators. The sale of Opium was connected in their minds with gambling, robbery, and false accusation; its special guilt consisted in its being a temptation to evil on the part of the salesmen, as the drug was destructive of the physical health, comfort, and life of their victims. The effects proved the criminality. Further, it was closely conjoined with various crimes already condemned in the statute book. It sprang up in a lawless locality at a great distance from Peking; there was therefore no inclination to leniency from the fear of offending persons or classes whom the Government would not like to offend. The law was in consequence promptly made, decided in tone, and severe in detail. Was this law acted upon? No allusion was made to it by the Jesuit missionaries in the *Lettres édifiantes* or in the *Mémoires concernant les Chinois.* The habit of Opium-smoking is not mentioned in these works. The trade in Opium certainly remained as before. 200 chests a year continued to be imported, and in 1767 that quantity had gradually increased to 1,000 chests. The duty was *Tk.* 3 a chest.* It would appear, then, that the old tariff of the MING dynasty was still followed in the main. The sale of Opium was prohibited by statute, but we do not find proof that it was refused as a drug at the Custom Houses of Amoy and Canton. The import steadily increased during the time it was in the hands of the Portuguese, till English merchants took it up in 1773, after the conquest of Bengal by CLIVE. The East India Company took the Opium trade into its own hands in 1781. At that time the minor portion only of the imported Opium was devoted to Opium-smoking—at least we may assume this. The Superintendents of Customs in those days would continue to take the duty on Opium as a drug. What was contraband they would say was *ya-pien-yen* (鴉 片 烟), which means Opium for smoking; the drug *ya-pien* would still pass the Customs as medicine. This seems to have been the reason that the import still continued to increase at about the same ratio as before the edict of A.D. 1729, not till after 40 years reaching a quantity amounting to 1,000 chests. Medicine claimed Opium as a most powerful agent, and since the commencement of the trade at Canton and Amoy, whether the merchants were Portuguese, Chinese, Arabs, or Dutch, it was as medicine that it had been sold. When DEFOE says of his hero in *Robinson Crusoe* that he went from the Straits to China in a ship with Opium, it was as a drug that he pictured it to

---

* The *Hai-kuo-t'u-chih* (海 國 圖 志), chapter 52, tells us that in 1662 the duty on Opium as a medical drug was *Tk.* 3 a picul, and that, beside this, *Tk.* 2 and 4 or 5 candareens were collected at a later period on each parcel, without saying what a parcel was. It is added that on account of the growth of Opium-smoking in the latter part of the eighteenth century, the Viceroy of Canton petitioned the Emperor to prohibit the importation, which was done in 1796.

himself.   Up to that time it was in fact a part of the trade in medicine; not long
after it became a trade in a drug used medically and for smoking combined.

28°.

The Native growth in Yünnan of the Opium Poppy can be traced to about
the same time, or a little later.   In the history of that province, published in 1736,
it is stated that Opium was then a common product of the department of Yung-
ch'ang-fu, in the western part of that province, where it borders on Burma.   It may
have been introduced by the Mahommedans, who were fond of it themselves, as a
powerful medicine, or it may have been brought there from Burma and Thibet.   It
is spoken of in the accounts we have of the trade of the sixteenth century as having
been introduced along with woven fabrics by traders coming from the coast of India.
Negapatam and Meliapur are mentioned as exporting both Opium and woven fabrics
to Pegu and Siam.   The seeds of the Poppy may therefore have been taken by the
Burmese route to Yünnan.   This Native Opium would be intended, not for Opium-
smoking, but to be used medically, as by a physician's prescription, or by the
contraction of a habit of daily consumption in a way like that of DE QUINCEY and
COLERIDGE.

The Mahommedans have long been a power in the province of Yünnan, and
their agency is to be suspected in this early cultivation of the Poppy in that part
of China.   It was they that first learned from the Greeks the wonderful soothing
powers of this drug.   They cultivated the Poppy in Arabia, then in Persia, then
in India.   It was from them, in the MING dynasty, that the Chinese learned the
way to cultivate the Poppy and derive the Opium juice from the capsules.   It was
they that carried on the trade in Opium, before the arrival of the Portuguese,
between the various sea-ports of the old Asiatic world.

It was probably by Mahommedan pilots that the ambassador of the MING
Emperor was conducted to the sea-ports of Arabia, Persia, and India in the voyage
we find on record.   It was through information given by Mahommedans residing
as merchants at Canton that the Portuguese were known by the Chinese historians

as *Faranggis* or Franks. It was because the Mahommedans wished to keep the profits of the trade in Opium and other articles exclusively to themselves that they prejudiced the Chinese Governors of Canton and Fuhkien against the Portuguese, and induced them to refuse the liberty to trade. We need not be surprised, therefore, if later on the cultivators of the Poppy in Yünnan, in the commencement of last century, were Mahommedans; they may have been simply the continuators of the MING dynasty cultivation, or they may have commenced afresh with seeds brought from Burma.

<h3 style="text-align:center">29°.</h3>

In the year 1742 an Imperial work on medicine was published under the name *I-tsung-chin-chien* (醫 宗 金 鑑). In this book, as a remedy for weak and injured lungs the capsules of the Poppy are directed to be used, with ginseng and apricot kernels, together with seven other medicines, prepared in the form of a decoction, to be drunk warm. Mention is also made of a Poppy ointment for scalds and burns. 15 Poppy flowers are to be used, and if not to be had, capsules are to be taken instead of them. A ditty of four lines in rhyme says that this ointment for burns and scalds is made with sesamum oil and Poppy flowers or capsules mixed with water and boiled down; white wax and true calomel are added. When smeared on the part affected the pain at once subsides. There is also a remedy for ulcers and tumours in which the capsules are used. It is a powder formed of olibanum and *huang-ch'i* (*Sophora tomentosa* or, say some, *Ptarmica Sibirica*,* a labiate plant used as a tonic). A ditty of four lines, used as a recipe, says that olibanum and *huang-ch'i* may be used for persons of a weak constitution who are afflicted with painful tumours and ulcers; such tumours if they have not grown to their full size will be at once dispersed, and if they are already mature they will break. The roots of *tang-kuei* (*Aralia edulis*), *shao-yao* (*Pæonia albiflora*), ginseng, *Sophora tomentosa*, *ch'uan-hsiung*,† and *Ti-huang* (comfrey, i.e., *Symphytum.*—WILLIAMS), together with olibanum, myrrh, Poppy capsules, and liquorice, are used to make this powder, which is also useful for bruises, sprains, wounds, and fractures.

Use of capsules in 1742.

* WILLIAMS's *Dictionary*, 蓍, page 346.
† *Hsiung* (芎) from Ssechwan. Belongs to *Levisticum*.

Present use of
capsules.

In addition to these recipes, there are several others in the same work which also contain the Poppy capsules. They are omitted for brevity. At present in Peking the capsules sold in drug shops are derived from the *Papaver somniferum*, cultivated at the town of An-su (near Pao-ting-fu), from Shansi, from Canton by sea, and from other places. They are bought and sold at the annual drug fair at Ch'i-chou, a city lying to the south-west of Pao-ting-fu.

30°.

Hoppo Book of
1753.

An account of the *Hoppo Book* of 1753 has been lately prepared by Dr. HIRTH and is printed in the *Journal of the China Branch of the Royal Asiatic Society* for the year 1882. The *Hoppo Book* is an explanation of the Custom House books in use at Canton in 1753 ; it was translated in that year, and contains varied information on the manner of settling the duties on all goods imported and exported at Canton. The author was an English merchant, whose name is not known. The division of the tariff is much the same as that of the present Chinese one, but imports and exports are not distinguished. Five kinds of taxes were then levied on Foreign trade :—

Five kinds of
duties in 1753.

I. An import duty, according to a fixed tariff, payable on all merchandise imported.

II. An export duty, payable on all exports, inclusive of re-exported goods proceeding to Ningpo and other ports on the Chinese coast ; it consisted of a tariff charge of 6 per cent. *ad valorem*.

III. Extra charges on exports and imports, such as for remitting the duty to Peking, for weighers, linguists, etc., and for servants of the Board of Revenue.

IV. Tonnage.

V. Present.

The three tariff
books.

The three books relating to the tariff at Canton which had then been authorised by the Board of Revenue at Peking are partly translated in this work, which also contains the manner of settling duties then in use at the port of Canton :—

    1st. *Chêng-hsiang-tsê-li*, or the book of true and fixed duties.

    2nd. *Pi-li*, or the book of comparisons.

    3rd. *Ku-chia*, or the book of valuation.

The first of these books was made A.D. 1687, and is kept as it was, unaltered. The book of comparisons was first sent, with about 150 articles collected together in it, to the Board of Revenue in Peking, for approval, in the year 1733. After this time every two or three years additional articles were added and sent to Peking for approval ; so that this book was continually increasing.

The third book is a register of the value of all goods exported or re-exported from Canton, for the purpose of laying on them an extra charge of 6 per cent., to be added to the other duty on such exports and re-exports.

Here we are astonished to find that in 1755 a picul of silk could be valued at   Prices ruling in Tls 100, and one of tea at Tls 8 ; that white sugar was worth Tls 1.50, brown sugar, 1755. Tls 1, sugar candy, Tls 2.50, rhubarb, Tls 1.50, per picul ; and that musk was valued at Tls 1.50 per catty ; while Opium was not worth more than half an ounce of silver per catty. The value of a chest of Opium would therefore amount at that time to not quite $100. The existence of Opium as an article of trade at Canton in the middle of last century is certainly beyond doubt; it is also mentioned in the KANG HSI tariff of 1687, and there pays a duty of 3 candareens per catty, constituting exactly 6 per cent. of the fixed value appearing in the valuation book.

31*.

In passing on to the year 1782 an extract may be here inserted from a letter, Opium-smuggling in 1782. dated 7th July 1782, of an official nature addressed from China by Mr. THOMAS FITZHUGH to Mr. GREGORY in London. It was presented to Parliament, and is taken from the *Commons' Report*, 1783, vol. vi.* " The importation of Opium to China is forbidden on very severe penalties : the Opium on seizure is burnt, the vessel in which it is brought to the port confiscated, and the Chinese in whose possession it is found for sale is punishable with death. It might be concluded that with a law so rigid no Foreigners would venture to import, nor any Chinese dare to purchase this article; yet Opium for a long course of time has been annually carried to China, and often in large quantities, both by our country's vessels and those of the Portuguese. It is sometimes landed at Macao and sometimes at Whampoa, though equally liable to the above penalties in either port, as the Portuguese are, so to say, entirely under the Chinese rule. That this contraband trade has hitherto been carried on without incurring the penalties of the law is owing to the excess of corruption in the executive part of the Chinese Government. . . . . In the year 1780 a new Viceroy was appointed to the government of Canton ; this man had the reputation of an upright, bold, and rigid Minister. I was informed that he had information of these illicit practices, and was resolved to take cognizance of them."

32°.

Opium-smoking in 1793.

England sent an Embassy in 1793, and China was minutely described by BARROW and STAUNTON. The habit of Opium-smoking had then been slowly growing for 60 years. Singularly, they only say when speaking of it that many of the higher mandarins took Opium ; they do not describe the mode of smoking. STAUNTON says, " They smoke tobacco mixed with other odorous substances, and sometimes a little Opium." Yet it cannot well be doubted that they referred to the habit of Opium-smoking. In the geographical work called *Hai-kuo-t'u-chih* we are told that Opium-smoking commenced only in the last years of the Emperor CHIEN LUNG, that is, about 1790. The explanation of this statement is found in the fact that it was only then that the habit reached Peking and became so general that public attention was called to it in Government documents. At about the same time the local

* Quoted in *Poppy Plague*, page 40, by J. F. B. TINLING.

authorities at Canton began to complain of rapid increase in the trade in Opium. In 1800 there was an edict issued prohibiting Opium from being brought to China in any ship. It was from this time that the more distinctly smuggling period commenced. It was a contraband trade, but connived at by Viceroys and Governors; they felt a difficulty, and concluded not to touch the evil with any firm intention to heal. How to treat it they knew not. The evil grew beyond their power of control. They regarded it as the "vile dirt of Foreign countries;" they feared it would spread among all the people of the inner land, wasting their time and destroying their property; they advocated the prohibition of the trade, and the Government consented to their advice, and frequently issued prohibitory edicts, but too often some of the officials themselves smoked, or their nearest friends smoked, and so the hand of interference was paralysed; and the demand for Opium continuing, the import was never seriously checked till the time of LIN Tsĕ-HSÜ and the war of 1841.

In 1800.

33°.

In the geographical work *Hai-kuo-t'u-chih* the following remarks also occur. In the year 1796 a prohibitory edict was received, but the official authorities at Canton still allowed Opium-receiving ships to anchor at Whampoa at a distance of only 4 English miles from the city. From this time smuggling proceeded year by year unchecked till 1822, when a local arrangement was decided on, according to the terms of which a charge was made of a regular amount on each chest; of this the officers, from the Viceroy downwards, whether civil or military, at the port connected with shipping all received a share. Most of this went to the office of the Superintendent. Some received it on board the ships, and others in the city of Canton. These sums were paid regularly month by month to the Chinese officers. In some cases Opium itself was given, instead of silver, in large and small portions. On each occasion of this kind one or more chests would be given, and sometimes as many as 150 chests. This irregular and illicit mode of proceeding lasted till the year 1840.

Statements in Hai-kuo-t'u-chih.

Local arrangement in 1822.

34°.

The following passage occurs in a botanical work, *Chih-wu-ming-shih-t'u-k'ao* (植 物 名 實 圖 考), published about 40 years ago :—"The Poppy is not mentioned before the T'ANG dynasty, A.D. 618 to 907. In the *Pen-ts'ao* of the period 968 to 976 the Poppy is placed in the lower division of cereal plants. In the SUNG dynasty a decoction of Poppy seeds was thought highly of, but at that time the medical efficacy of the capsules and seeds was understood to extend only, as being astringent, to the cure of diarrhœa and dysentery. In the MING dynasty, 1368 to 1644, the pill called *I-li-chin-tan*, or golden elixir, came into use, and was found to be very deleterious if much was taken. Of late years Opium has spread throughout the Empire—a universal poison. Its effects are as bad as those of the poisonous plant known by the name *Tuan-ch'ang-ts'ao*, as producing internal rupture in the intestines. Yet as the guilt is not in the flower, it finds its place in botanical works on flowers."

35°.

Mr. DONALD SPENCE, British Consul at Ch'ung-ch'ing-fu, in Szechwan, in the year 1881, made inquiries into the amount of Opium produced at that time in the four south-western provinces. He states that in Szechwan the consumption of Native Opium within the province amounts to 54,000 piculs, while 123,000 piculs are sent to other provinces ; of these, 70,000 piculs are exported in an easterly direction, 40,000 piculs paying duty, and 30,000 piculs being smuggled. Yünnan produces annually 35,000 piculs, and Kweichow 10,000 piculs, while Hupeh supplies to the market not more than 2,000 piculs. In all, the production of Native Opium amounts to 224,000 piculs. Mr. SPENCE's Report on the Native production of Opium was forwarded to the Foreign Office of the British Government, and was subsequently presented to Parliament and printed. If a comparison be made of the amount of Opium produced in the four above-mentioned provinces, viz., 224,000 piculs, with the quantity of Foreign Opium imported in 1882, viz., 66,900 piculs, it will be seen that the Opium of Native production is more than three times as much in quantity as that introduced from India and elsewhere.

36°.

In Mr. TINLING's *Poppy Plague* there are 75 pages of closely printed in- Concluding note.
formation on the history of British Opium, chiefly collected from the Parliamentary
Papers of 1783, 1787, 1831, and 1840, and from the East India Company's Reports
of 1812 and 1813. The present Historical Note is made up of information from
the Chinese side and from KÆMPFER, who is not alluded to by the authors of the
Poppy Plague and *Our Opium Policy*.

INDEX.

罌粟源流考

II.—SPECIAL SERIES.

罌粟源流考

罌粟源流考

罌粟花一物拉丁文種花卉之古書中屢見史傳中亦常道及有羅馬人哥尼

流尼波斯所著之書云羅馬王達耳貴尼欲取伊都利亞國之一城時先以詭

計毒撻世子世子負傷奔入彼城彼城人咸以為王子必深恨其父終不能父

子相睦矣遂立之為統領冀其掌兵權以抗父也詎知王子反覆尋計終欲將

城歸其父哉奈以不獲善策遂遣人詣父於花園發操刀將

罌粟花之鮮艷高大者斷數株示使人使人歸語諸世子會悟父意將將

中顧宦數人復婉言勸諭城中黎庶使奉其父為國主此中國周敬王時事

也

希臘國詩家和美耳亦曾道及罌粟花其詩集載者有如是一事適敵人某向

希哥多耳戰鬪敵人發來一矢未中希哥多耳身射中其弟之胸弟遂負痛垂

頸和美耳賦詩形容其勢謂宛如罌粟花放於園中向旁側欲首沾濃露低垂

其葳蕤之狀與重盈冠頂力不能勝相似創始希臘國將罌粟汁歸入藥品謂

其能醫治疾病者為希臘拉低斯乃中國周威烈王考王安王相繼在位時

人也希臘醫家奉其書為醫學之宗凡植物之汁希臘語均呼為阿伯斯呼罌

粟為美根後變音總呼為阿比恩原為希臘語也拉丁語亦如是呼之雖希

波草拉低斯書中未嘗有是名去其時未久泰西醫士通以阿比恩為定名矣

拉丁詩家韋而吉利詩中恒有提及罌粟花之語讚其令人多眠亦讚其令人

忘憂旆讚其宛同幽冥地府之利低河死者由其河經過倬其將在世生活時

之一應事俱不記憶乃藉用希臘人俗傳死後欲利低河水忘前世之語也韋

而吉利將罌粟花比擬幽冥地府利低河之外復屢言其為屬於司穀女神吉

利斯之罌粟花緣希臘國以石雕刻出司穀神之女像手持有罌粟花枝也由

來臆度之家推測司穀神所以手持罌粟花之故所論不同有謂一日女神出

遊至一家暫憩彼家欲授之粲女神竊知其孩童有疾遂外出為採罌粟花一

掬命彼家製而和乳飼孩童己食若許孩童愈己乃不覺腹餓人故誌之者

有謂罌粟為麥田野花以其與麥同生故持之者或又有謂罌粟花色白食之者

于能令人增食量伊古來賜人五穀百果即此司穀之女神者據公理而論古

人見麥田中諸野花之豔麗美觀無出罌粟花之右者故令司穀女神手中持

一罌粟花枝也韋而吉利著之書即在中國前漢時至東漢中葉復有百利尼

著之動植金石物通考一書也更有希臘醫家丟斯哥利低斯

著之萬種藥料集成一書二書中均著有阿扁能安人心神止疼使人多眠獲

安之各種功效

中國隋唐之世亞拉伯人自立為大食國於代宗廣德元年時建都於底哥利

斯河旁巴哥大低城呼其王之語曰加利佛伊等極重希臘醫學醫治各種疾

病即用希臘人之法並希臘人所用之各種藥各藥中阿扁亦在內亞拉伯人

遂將扁音之在幫母下音若者變入於非母下音若芙蓉巴耳西亞人則變入於並

母下音成片是以有阿芙蓉阿片二呼稱也細考夫亞拉伯並巴耳西亞語按

其意均有是種花之名是其二國於古昔由來應有是花矣因其顏色美艷故

而珍重寶貴至歸入藥品之大用乃後時由希臘國傳來之法也

按中國自漢初與南越通關市而互市之制行焉北魏立互市於南陲及宋開

寶四年置市舶司於廣州杭明州等處首即先言大食通貨

大食國於唐宋時來中國通商故亞拉伯人航海至廣州等處海口携來象牙

乳香寶鐵綿花白龍腦白沙糖琉璃器薔薇水等貨並各種藥材相與交易醫

藥亦或在藥材中揀厥情形彼時之先中國殆未嘗有罌粟花也伊等並著明

其在藥品中爲安心神增飲食令人多眠之物見其所結之寶如罌其子如米

色不同而大小相若故呼之曰米囊

按唐開海舶西域回教默德那國王謨罕驀德遣其母舅番僧蘇哈白窠來中

土貿易建光塔及懷聖寺告成壽雙遂葬於此（見番禺縣志）即明史所載鄭和所至

之阿丹詧考之順紅海東濱北去二千七八百里即默德那地謨罕驀德死

於貞觀六年

唐明皇時陳藏器述罌陽子言曰罌粟花有四葉紅白色上有淺紅暈子其囊形

如鵪頭箭中有細米

考之是時大食人之往來中國已足百載而罌粟花有不同薔薇茉莉在中國

地遍種者乎前三百餘年亞拉伯人已將耶悉茗指甲花茉莉帶來

唐郭橐駝種樹書云鶯粟九月九日及中秋夜種之花必大于必滿　見圖書集成博物彙編草

木典鶯粟郎　彙考並花郎

按郭橐駝家於長安城西豐樂鄉沒後柳宗元爲作傳約爲盛唐時人觀此即

知罌粟在彼時於彼處如何矣

唐雍陶西歸出斜谷詩云　行過嶮棧出褒斜歷盡平川似到家萬里客愁今日

散馬前初見米囊花　雍陶爲四川成都人可知彼時其處已有罌粟花也

由唐至德至宋乾德二百年內大食人來中國者中國書籍離不曾多載而其

時有二大食人紀載之遊華日記遜來譯爲西文是未嘗斷夫往來也罌粟可

充藥品殆亦大食人所告知者故開寶本草即嘗其可醫病矣

宋太祖開寶六年命尙藥奉御劉翰道士馬志等九人參訂開寶本草呼罌粟曰

罌子粟一名米嚢子又名御米並言其米主治丹石毒勸不下飮食和竹瀝煮作

粥食極美

宋蘇軾詩云　道人勸飮鶏蘇水童子能煎鶯粟湯

[v]

宋蘇轍種藥苗詩有云

築室城西中有圃書窗戶之餘松竹扶疏枝棘開唯以

毓嘉蔬唯夫告子罌粟可儲罌小如罌粟細如粟與麥皆熟苗堪春菜

實比秋穀研作牛乳烹為佛粥老人氣衰飲食無幾食肉不消食菜寞味柳鎚石

鉢熒以蜜水便口利喉調肺簧門三年杜門莫適往還幽人衲僧相對忘言飲之

一杯失笑欣然我來潁川如遊廬山

宋仁宗詔天下郡縣圖上所產藥物用唐高宗命英國公等修成英公唐本草故

事專命太常博士蘇頌述成圖經本草其書中云罌粟花處處有之人多蒔以

為飾花有紅白二種微哐氣其實形如瓶子有米粒極細圍人隔年糞地九月布

子涉冬至春始生苗極繁茂不爾則不生生亦不茂俟黃乃采之又云治反

胃吐食有罌粟粥用白罌粟米三合人參末三大錢生山芋五寸細切研三物以

水二升三合炎取六合入生薑汁及罌花少許和匀分服亦無妨別服

湯九士自書契以來經史九流百家之說至於圖緯律呂星官算法山經本草無
所通
宋史蘇頌列傳言其器局閎遠不與人校短長以禮法自持雖貴養如寒

按康熙年間德國醫士甘伯佛耳曾奉瑞典君主達派隨使臣至巴耳西亞言

及彼處出阿片之罌粟乃放白花者可恍然於蘇頌時雖阿片之名尚未著於

書要已有可出阿片之白罌粟花也而英國植物著名家林得利亦云可製阿

片之罌粟卽紅花黑子者一種白花白子者一種

宋徽宗政和中醫官通直郎寇宗奭讚本草衍義其書中云其華亦有千葉者一

五

六

礬凡數千萬粒大小如葶藶子而色白其米性寒多食利二便勤膀胱氣屬石人

研此水煮加礬作湯飲之甚宜

宋林洪山家清供中有罌乳魚云將罌粟淨洗磨乳先以小粉置紅底用絹裹濾

乳下之去清入釜稍沸匙瀝淡醋收聚仍入囊壓成塊乃以小粉飯內下乳燕熟

豎以紅麴水瀝又少燕取出起作魚片即罌粟魚 見圖 書 集成 至是爲用粟穀之始林

洪殆南宋人乎

宋謝薖罌粟花七言絶句　鉛膏細細點花梢道是春深雪未消一斛千囊蒼玉

粟東風吹作米長腰芳 見廣 羣

即李時珍依次援引書法臆度之以粟穀醫病疑自南宋時始後之楊王二君

其殆亦南宋人也既未載明法由中國何人創用蓋亦由於西方人傳來緣西

方人由來以粟穀爲醫病之妙藥也

宋將末時楊士瀛直指方云粟穀治痢人皆諱之固矣然下痢日久腹中無積痛

當止澀者登容不有此劑何以對治乎但要有轉佐耳

宋王璆之百一選方中治泄痢赤白用罌粟子炒罌穀炙等分爲末煉蜜丸梧

于大每服三十九米飲下有人輕驗

宋王碩易簡方云粟穀治痢如神但性緊澀多令嘔逆故人畏而不敢服若令醋

制加以烏梅則用得法矣或同四君子藥尤不致閉胃妨食而獲奇功也

金劉河間宣明方治欬嗽多年自汗者用罌粟殼二兩半去蒂膜醋炒取一兩烏

梅半兩焙爲末每服二錢臥時白湯下

元李杲云罌粟殼收歛固氣能入腎故治骨病尤宜 李杲號東垣元時明醫受業於張元素

元危亦林得效方治久泄不止粟殼去筋蜜炙爲末每服五分蜜湯下穀氣素壯

人用之卽效

元朱震亨曰今人虛勞欬嗽多用粟殼止刦及濕熱泄痢者用之止澀其治病之

功雖急殺人如劍宜深戒之又云治欬嗽多用粟殼不必疑但要先去病根此乃收

后藥也治痢亦同凡痢須先散邪行滯豈可遽投粟殼龍骨之藥以閉塞腸胃邪

氣得補而愈甚所以變症作而淹延不已也 朱震亨字彥修號丹溪元史有彼之列傳旣云殺人如劍可決其爲出鴉

片之罌粟殺矣

元馮子振十八公賦云 或簇烘霧之罌粟或戴凝霜之菊英

明周定王橚之普濟方治熱痢便血粟殼醋炙一兩陳皮半兩爲末每服三錢烏

梅湯下

前明之初中國已與印度亞拉伯南洋羣島尚夫往來依指南針方向航海行

船幾足三百載於宜和四年徐兢使高麗卽商務漸盛兼以巴耳西亞人奉 視指南浮針方向乘船而往者

爲國主者與元朝同宗族戀遷交易之事益以多矣是以永樂皇帝卽位屢遣

鄭和乘舟航海越南洋羣島西至阿丹地卽紅海南口今茲往來中西之輪帆

七

恒憩息處也並至忽魯謨斯地卽巴耳西亞海灣之海口出入處印度東西海

濱各地至者亦不乏所謂小葛蘭古里柯枝等國殆卽印度西鄙之貫倫哥貝

加利古德也若許地面之土產爲能不爲粵東商人販運乎各國之善經商者

推囘囘人爲最中國人次之鄭和率兵至彼處於中國戰貨之商船均可有保

護照應赴各地貿易者殆可增多也弘治十一年時佛郎機人初次至柯枝

一面理商務一面征服其各地不數年間凡阿丹忽魯謨斯哥

亞古里柯枝小葛蘭直他海口爲己之屬地於佛郎機矣伊等窩或事於商

事囘教人所居之各處俱屬於彼有葡萄亞人佛郎機卽巴耳波撒著之書云

販貨物赴滿剌加者爲囘教人前他教之人均帶阿片至滿剌加處與在彼遇

之中國商船交易且云亞拉伯地出之阿片運至印度西濱加利古德亦有由

甘拜帶至加利古德者甘拜去現出小洋藥之馬拉瓦甚近

由是觀之甘拜殆爲由來可炮製阿片之處所也光緒八年進口來之洋藥六

萬五千七百擔中有馬拉瓦小洋藥二萬九千三百擔甘拜或卽明史中之甘

巴里也

明成化時王璽著之醫林集要云阿芙蓉是天方圜種紅罌粟花不令水淹頭七

八月花謝后剌青皮取之者又云以阿芙蓉小豆許窒心溫水化下日一鳳

㕘葱蒜漿水若渴飮寳水解之又云鴉片治久痢不止罌粟花花卿結殼後三五

日午後於觳上用大鍼刺開外面靑皮十餘處次日早津出以竹刀刮在磁器內

陰乾每用小豆大一粒空心溫水化下忌葱蒜漿水如熱渴以蜜水解之

按明史王璽列傳謂其鎭守甘肅二十餘年回敎人所居之哈密土魯番等處

物產醫術習俗自必熟悉故可將阿芙蓉事言之鑿鑿也

適於王璽論阿芙蓉後不數年至弘治年間葡萄亞人（卽佛郎機人）法斯哥得加馬

至印度之柯枝等處壓罌粟製爲鴉片之法回敎人與印度人習熟已久也印度

東西海濱均有炮製鴉片事以備商船戀遷由印度赴緬甸暹羅之東海濱一

帶設置坊作亦不乏伊等運貨至各地交易時此種物亦在其中無不可携而

至於中國之廣州廈門等處也

嘉靖二十六年佛郞機（卽葡亞船）載貨泊浯嶼時漳泉賈人往貿易焉巡海使者柯

喬發兵攻其船而販者不止都御史朱紈獲通販九十餘人斬之通都海禁漸肅

迨隆慶元年福建巡撫都御史塗澤民請開海禁

東西洋考云朱時發舶海上郡國有司臨水送之營登泉山見刻石紀歲月甚夥

爾時典章重云閩在宋元俱設市舶司國初因之後竟廢成弘之際豪門巨室間

有乘巨艦貿易海外者奸人陰開其利竇而官人不得顯收其利權初亦漸享奇

腹久乃弓引爲亂矣又云海濱一帶田盡斥鹵耕者無所望歲只有視淵若陵久

成習慣富家徵貨固得稇載而來貧者爲傭亦博升米自給一旦戒嚴不得下水

九

[x]

断其生活若輩悉健有力勢不肯搏手困寶於是所在連結為亂潰裂以出其久

潛踪於外者既觸網不敢歸又連結遠人郡導以入矣惟有關海禁徵商稅以及

買舶固始因以裕民始頏以安而歲額兵餉方藉以充其時徵稅之規有

水餉有加增餉水餉者以船廣狹為準其餉出於船商陸餉者以貨多寡

計值徵輸其餉有差則禁船商無先起貨以餉商接買貨應

稅之數給號票就船完餉而後聽其轉運為其所云加增餉者殆即船之尺丈

而量加減也又萬曆十七年提督軍門周嘉允陸餉貨物抽稅則例沒藥乳香阿

魏等貨每百斤均有稅銀定數外阿片每十斤稅銀二錢至四十三年貨物抽稅

現行則例阿片每十斤稅銀一錢七分三釐矣

明李挺醫學入門中云鴉片一名阿芙蓉即罌粟花未開時用竹鍼刺十數孔其

津自出次日以竹刀刮在磁器內待積取多了以紙封固曬二七日即成片矣性

急不可多用又云治虛痢及久痢一切諸痢用黃連四兩以吳茱萸水浸炒木

香一兩阿芙蓉一錢右為末陳米糊和九菉豆大每二三十九以蓮肉煎湯吞下

被盍就睡奏效神矣　見東醫寶鑑

李挺乃正德嘉靖時人嘉靖二年日本人掠中國海濱中國遂罷市舶嚴海禁

外洋貨物不得入口故李挺特群言由罌粟花中探取鴉片法也

明龔雲林醫鑑云治赤白痢下用鴉片木香黃連白朮各一分研末飯九小豆大

壯者一分老幼半分空心米飲下忌酸物生冷油膩茶酒麴無不止者口渴署飲

十

米湯又方罌粟花未開時外有兩片青葉包之花開卽落收取爲末每米飲服一

錢神效赤痢用紅花者白痢用白花者此以葉醫病法爲他人所未言及更有可治二十四種病

症之一方治何症以何等藥湯送下名其丸曰一粒金丹法卽用眞阿芙蓉一分

梗米飯搗作三九每服一丸未效再進一丸不可多服忌醋令人腸斷伊之萬病

回春書中云一粒金丹治氣痛以阿芙蓉卽鴉片二錢半阿魏一錢木香沉香各

五分牛黄二分半先將沉香木香牛黄爲末以鴉片阿魏放碗內滴水銚化和蜜

爲丸菉豆大金箔爲衣每一粒熱氣痛凉水下冷氣痛滾水下神效彼復有牛黄

紫金丹所用以佐阿芙蓉之藥品乃大同小異見本草綱目并東醫寶鑑

明李時珍本草綱目云罌粟寶狀如罌子其米如粟乃象乎穀而可以供御故有

御米象穀諸名又云罌粟秋種冬生嫩苗作蔬食甚佳葉如白苣三四月抽薹結

青苞花開則苞脫花凡四瓣大如仰盞罌在花中鬚蕊裹之花開三日卽謝而罌

在莖頭長一二寸大如馬兜鈴上有蓋下有蒂宛然如酒罌中有白米極細可煮

粥和飯食水研濾漿同綠豆粉作腐食尤佳亦可取油其殼入藥甚多而本草不

載乃知古人不用之也宋人卽言北江東人呼千葉者爲麗春花或謂是罌粟別種蓋

亦不然其花變態本自不常有白者紅者紫者粉紅者杏黄者半紅者半紫者半

白者豔麗可愛故曰麗春又曰賽牡丹曰錦被花詳見遊獸齋花譜又謂其米治

瀉痢潤燥謂其殼以水洗潤去蒂及筋膜取外薄皮陰乾細切以米醋拌炒入藥

十一

亦有蜜炒蜜炙者氣味酸濇微寒無毒得醋烏梅橘皮良止瀉痢固脫肛治遺精久欬歛肺濇腸止心腹筋骨諸痛又云阿芙蓉俗作鴉片名義未詳或云阿方音稍我也以其花色似芙蓉而得此名并云阿芙蓉前代罕聞近方有用者云是罌粟花之津液也罌粟結青苞時午后以大針刺其外面青皮勿惧裏面硬皮或三五處次早津出以竹刀刮收入瓷器陰乾用之故今市者猶有苞片在內氣味酸濇溫微毒治潤痢脫肛不止能濇丈夫精氣俗人房中術用之京師僧一粒金丹云通治百病會方伎家之術耳

明萬曆年間王世懋之花疏云芍藥之後罌粟花最繁華其物能變加意灌植妍好千態曾有作黃色綠色者遠視佳甚近不堪聞其粟可爲腐濇精物也　見圖書集成

明吳幼培罌粟花詩　庭院深沉白晝長塔前仙卉吐靈芳含烟帶雨呈嬌艷傳粉凝脂遷艷妝種自中秋須隔歲開於初夏伴傾陽更誇結子纍纍碩何必汗邪滿稻粱　見廣羣芳譜

明高濂草花譜云罌粟花有千瓣五色虞美人瓣短而嬌滿園春夾瓣飛勤春以子種　見圖書集成

明末園初時之物理小識書云罌粟中秋午種花後囊如瓶有細米可粥可以取油其囊入藥主濇欲其結青苞時以鍼劃十數眼其津液自出收入瓷器用紙封口暴二七日即成鴉片最能濇精

觀前數段乃知前明成化以來中國已有內地出之鴉片矣非止今日分外來

洋藥本地煙土也觀書者宜詳閱之惟李時珍所引紅罌粟花為天方國種七

八月後採取東醫寶鑑云治久痢不止罌粟花卻結殼後三五日可取其津均

為由王璽之醫林集要摘來同一人同一書也於彼則明言天方於此則若隨

處可取殆書一而所引之處不一也故李時珍有方土有異之說矣

前明崇禎年間和蘭國醫士本丟斯久居於咬𠺕吧地巴大非亞城至崇禎二年

壽終於彼平素所記錄見聞事實有一契友為收拾起越二十九年擺印成書行

於世其書中云亞細亞洲諸國凡吞服鴉片者極似恒在睡鄉無精神經理貿易

無氣力與人戰爭惟醫士治疾於天氣炎熱之區不用鴉片為難一切霍亂瘟疫

中暑瀉痢并肝氣等症時而多有治此諸病俱宜以鴉片為君并云咬𠺕吧人民

貧寒之家將罌粟之花葉枝莖等製次等鴉片備用富有厚貲者方服用上品鴉

片彼又云古昔希臘國人第知鴉片害人之嗹不知其醫疾各妙用以其未嘗考

究至精細處也且本丟斯自與人醫病無論遇瀉痢霍亂疫癘以及羊癇瘋與中

風各等症均依賴乎鴉片時間或用罌粟殼罌粟子更自言其以鴉片為人治肺氣虛損諸疾曾有

用紅花佐鴉片成功宛如船之賴鐵錨然為人醫疾雖施之與

嬰童亦無受傷處緣嚴謹慎審不使溢應用之分也

十四

至明代將終吞服之鴉片將變為吸食之鴉片矣著錄至此不能不以黃烟為

導引也

黃烟一物原為美國土產明將末時傳入中國者也火著之而吸其烟亦始於

美國土人西班亞人學得其種植吸食法由海舶越大東洋而攜至呂宋呂宋

即福建漳州泉州南海中之大島也馬尼喇城即其海口之大埠頭種黃烟極

盛其時華人呼烟草為淡巴姑美國原名曰多巴哥明史呼居呂宋之西班亞

人為佛郎機人居澳門之蒲都家麗人亦呼為佛郎機人其實佛郎機乃回教

人呼歐羅巴人之通稱也唐時華人呼歐羅巴人為佛林即綠從回教人之呼

稱而呼之也

物理小識書云萬曆末有攜淡巴姑烟草至漳泉者馬氏造之曰淡肉果蕭傳至

九邊皆喘長簪而火點吞吐之有醉仆者崇禎時嚴禁之不止其本似春不老而

葉大於茱暴乾以火酒炒之曰金絲烟北人呼為淡巴姑或呼擔不歸可以祛濕

發撒然久服則肺焦諸藥多不效其症忽吐黃水而死

於黃烟傳入中國內地時亦曾傳至英國英君主雅各第一痛罵吸食之風

不可行也曾著書疾其物并勸諭國民不可食亦萬曆末年事也

崇德六年上諭王貝勒大臣曰爾等何不親率人習射耶子弟壯者當令以角弓

羽箭幼者以木弓柳箭我國武功首重習射不習射之罪非用烟可比用烟之禁

前因爾等私用故不能治人至於射藝切不可荒廢嗣後嚴加督率爲是見東華錄彼

時之王貝勒大臣等私用黃烟不能禁人之用者今日之王貝勒大臣等果無私

用鴉片者乎

尊鄉贅筆中云明季服烟有禁惟閩人幼而習之他處百無一二也近日賓主相

見以此鳴敬倪仰涕唾惡態畢具則城市服之已而沿及鄉村矣始猶男子服

之既則徧滿閨閣矣習俗移人眞有不知其然而然者即此觀之乃知中國人沾

染嗜好之易傳開矣至嘉慶道光之時鴉片亦如黃烟之傳遍通國儒家雖鄙而

惡之總不能使之中止國家縱嚴爲禁之終未嘗使之盡絕黃烟之無益於人未

嘗至初逆料者之若等大鴉片之爲患於人較人所初逆料者大數倍也無論其

爲患大小殆非國家禁止斷絕之易事耳

德國醫士甘伯佛耳於康熙三十二年由巴耳西亞國即唐之波斯國之咬𠺕吧日本回歸著

成之書中有云巴耳西亞國人因阿片能增人喜樂使人得安也故呼之爲提利

亞吉提利亞吉希臘語意即能醫病之藥也伊處人於初夏探取罌粟汁漿法

即以五利刃刀縱橫刺其罌頭之半面薄皮一刺薄皮面即有五乳次日汁漿浸

出以片刀刮下收入器中其器懸於胸下有腰帶繫之也繼復以五利亦刀刺罌

頭彼半面薄皮依舊之次日收其汁漿罌頭大小不等有先長足者有後長

足者如是之經營操作須費數日工方能畢乃事也設一株之枝條過多先伐其

十五

旁出之柔條獨留其居中之巨莖如是爲之疆頭可期肥大中藏之汁可有大力

初次採取之汁漿佳於末次採取者且體重色白亮或亦有透灰色者貯器內屬

時愈久質愈乾時色愈暗也二次採之汁漿色暗於初次者彷彿紅黑色亦有三

採其汁漿者乃色甚黑而力極寡矣

巴耳西亞炮製阿片法所極緊要者卽於其汁漿中兌少許水滋潤之也滴入水

後傾於平底盤中以厚木匙來去往復調和之務展長其工至其汁漿漸成爲

黑而膠黏起光亮仿如稀香之質而止更以手搓和匀停團爲球輭入短筒中提

入市而售與人醃人膳之多寡刀剪下而零售炮製阿片時或有不和以水而用

白蜂蜜代之者取其不惟可袪乾燥兼能滅苦味也復有於炮製時加以性皮葚

蔻花白荳蔻等藥品細末者伊等謂其於心神幷腦漿有益也

剛有一類炮製阿片之人伊等不用香品藥料止用西藏紅花與琥珀二味合阿

片成九有若許人緣自已服用不假市肆人手在家自修合矣恐於配合他物時

市肆人或有失多失寡之欺罔也第上所言之三種炮製法均爲將阿片合爲九

以水送服也外復有釀就之阿片水可以供飲伊圍名之曰哥哥那耳周初時希

臘人和笑耳之詩中名爲尼本低斯飲其水者俱有一定時刻飲多飲寡亦有一

定分兩或向行店購取或於家中自置均無不可亦有人取罌粟花葉加水置慢

火上熏熬安而飲之更有人將罌粟殼研碎安置酒漏形之淋于上澆以水運七

八次倒罡淋之至欲加以何等香品藥料惟視乎飲其水者之意斟酌量用之耳

復有一事阿片凡吞服入腹可令人倖狂喜怒仿如飲酒至醉之分位究厭由來

即以阿片爲之甚也其他等爲佐之藥料或由醫士意或由己之意順便加入堪

爲阿片輔佐之藥不乏大抵以助氣力養心神爲本也其內最著名之一品凡名

曰哈斯冶莫伯吉即言能令人心生喜樂飄飄欲仙體輕儼同於騰雲駕霧而在

天上坐也

歐羅巴人用阿片醫病也每次止一哥蘭（五哥蘭約一分）問或用二三四哥蘭踰此分

兩人將視以爲必至死而巴耳西亞與相接壞昆連之國不然習用多年縱用六

十哥蘭（約一錢半）爲一劑吞服亦不至死其處可如是之多服阿片年深日久爲害

孔多致人身體瘦形神困億心氣鬱悶聰明靈性變愚蠢由旁觀之見其仿如

欲眠之木椿瘦前緘默不語知爲有阿片癖之客若等人恒有就予前望予

助彼戒除阿片引者曾有人重懸賞格謂誰能救予脫離阿片苦處願以百枚金

錢持贈倘予能挽廻彼之沉淪使其不至喪失予即可得其謝金無靈人之吞服

阿片矣諸國醫士所著之書中論道吞服阿片者之苦楚極詳余茲時無勞多贅

猶有可述之一事即有人二月間取罌粟嫩殼存之米醋中以備不時之需也甘

伯佛耳由巴耳西亞啟行曾至閣婆卽今之咬𠺕吧也卽晋時法顯至之耶婆

提東西洋考名曰加留巴彼地之黑皮土人有助兒橫增氣力壯臍量之惡法或

遭遇不嘉自思無趣不欲生活世間也或受人凌辱欲輕已之生藉以洩憤復讐

也法卽存服阿片九阿片九入腹倏忽之間可勃然震怒增益千萬倍殘忍暴虐

之氣識見而不醒人事絕非理法所能繩東遂致手執利刃形如猛虎直向人

烟闌熱之處往狂奔路遇之人無論為素相友者或素所讐者舉可殺剗亦或輕他

人乘勢掫倒此等情形彼土人民間人以哈木哥在咬𠺕吧與相近彼處之各海島時

常見之彼土人呼為哈木哥之語大聲呼也俱有驚懼意望而見之者莫

不應麑亦以哈木哥疾呼殺人者至醫人之未帶防身兵器者速趨避其

兒鋒其携有制人器械者宜火速來前處死此哈木哥人也

甘伯佛耳書又云咬𠺕吧黑人於吞服黃煙之外復有一遞黃煙用阿片之法先取

水入阿片中攪和勻以是阿片水抖黃煙意卽取其能使頭眩腦熱志氣昏惰而

多生喜樂也伊井云咬𠺕吧地有處於孔道旁搭蘆棚以阿片水所調和之黃

煙待客有於其途輕過者招之使吸諭及貿易中之獲利與盛百貨之中南洋諸

國無出巴大非亞咬𠺕吧大城鴉片一宗有者服食慣者不能令其中止不屬巴大

非亞商船由印度之榜葛拉（卽佛經所言之中印度亦卽乾隆年間英國所取之）

卽大洋藥也（戴回之貨中有阿片井由印度東海濱之哥羅滿拉亦帶回阿片也）

甘伯佛耳論黃煙云於前百有五十年間由漸盛行於天下各國凡亞細亞地厥

羅巴地亞非利加地幾於無處不吸黃煙也巴耳西亞有黃煙之初卽由葡萄亞

十八

人帶者各地俱呼之爲多巴哥緣西印度有名爲多巴哥之島嶼所出之煙草甚

多故以其島名名其草也此煙草在藥中爲有毒者類嘗見平素未曾吸慣之

人初次吸烟草非頭疼卽嘔吐亦或心作煩悶執此卽可斷其爲毒草類矣奚必

援他據乎更取煙草之汁漿少許敷於鷚鳥之破傷處頭之鷚鳥卽死人身有破

損處塗之亦不穩妥余於俄國之嘎三城見肩擔物者數人於面穿孔之牛角內

貯以煙草蒅就火上燃著而吸吞其煙及吸盡遂倒地口流痰涎儼若羊癎瘋狀

煙草蒅雖屬有毒及化爲煙而供人吸食吸用熟慣不惟於人無損反於人增加

利益能使人頭腦清爽倍加喜樂巴耳西亞人欲多得舒適快樂故於吸食時用

一特製之器如圖〔見英文中〕製成玻璃器貯水至大半滿以火吸煙煙中縱有硫磺與

他等物於腦髓有損有此番水中經歷吸其氣味吸入腹亦歸清涼淨潔無所謂

毒物含於內矣名其器曰卡連乃玻璃瓶形體高五寸腹大頸長頂問覆以銅冒

空球圓直徑寸半或二寸不等任一管較長直入瓶內水面下此

管上端有盛黃煙之玲瓏剔透煙形如酒漏或喇叭之鍋滿裝煙蒅於鍋中上置

木炭引火彼一管較短下端不及水面上端旁彎納入人手持之長管端中烟蒅

火化之烟卽可由玻璃瓶串入長管達至人口也設娜烟草之味過苦可先於水

中浸泡泡法製出其味苦之汁漿余見中國人日本國人俱有如是泡製者此等吸

黃烟之法乃巴耳西亞人所初創居印度亞拉伯人幷印度人亦效尤南洋羣島

之黑人習回教時亦相習成風且伊等無玻璃器乃以葫蘆等依式製造代玻璃

用矣凡中國人土耳其人日本人俱如西人之式以管吸黃烟下端有裝烟之銅

黑皮土人吸烟不以管烟葉捲成卷口含一端彼一端火燃而已

麻之一物南洋諸島不乏巴耳西亞亦多有性能令人增歡樂種子嘗粉皆可用

葉更佳巴耳西呼麻葉製成之水日榜將其葉浸泡凉水內釀之其所釀之水

假同酒醉生出極大歡樂出門人腰間俱帶麻葉亦帶可製麻葉水之輕器法即

先以麻葉一掬納水中潤沃之從將水澄出止存深淨碎麻葉復注水以手輕

揉之仍去其水存麻葉艑乃以杵研成細膩糊於是徐徐酌清水

於上更以杵研數分鐘遂傾於布上瀘淋其水水力甚大存於布上之粗渣滓

遺棄不用每炮製一次一人可分得能容半升之一碗水但宜不停手之攪和恐

水內所含麻之細末沉碗底大衆一同暢飲於同時與發歡樂亦有不兌合水

止將其研成之細膩糊爲九服之者印度人呼常服此物之人爲榜吉臺灣志云

鴉片土同麻切蘇殆取其克助精神增快樂耳

英國人名爲低佛者有著書才曾盧擬夫喜乘槎至各地貿易者末後獨居荒島

創成蔥室輕種之一切事集成一書攔印於康熙五十九年內有云其人由南霎

島乘貿易船赴中國所載貨之最要者惟有鴉片

雍正初年間年希堯序之集驗良方中有萬應丹一方卽以鴉片和牛黃冰片等

十三味藥配成治一切四時傷寒瘟疫中暑風痰頭疼身熱吐瀉痢瘧心腹疼等

症重者二丸輕者一丸冷水下又有痲眞膏一方專貼臍上能固精保元煖腎補

腰膝去寒濕一切腹痛并他等男婦諸症法即以鴉片麝香歸起石乳香丁香等

復和他藥十四味熬煉成膏隨時取用更有一洞府保養靈龜神方亦顋以鴉片

蟾酥等和他等藥三十三品兌油熬成者觀此知鴉片於彼時中國醫家猶視爲

益人者多也

宛平黃玉圃之臺海使槎錄云鴉片烟用麻葛同鴉土切絲於銅鑑內煮成鴉片

拌烟另用竹箕實以菱絲聚吸之索值數倍於常烟專治此者名開鴉片舘吸

一二次後便刻不能離暖氣直注丹田可竟夜不眠土人服此爲導淫具肢體萎

縮臟腑潰出不殺身不止官弁每爲嚴禁常有身被建擊猶求緩須臾再吸一筒

者鴉片土出咬𠺕吧 即加 留吧

以竹箕吸食鴉片之事他書雖有記載惟此臺海使槎錄最詳至其書爲何年

著成未審考究得惟於乾隆十一年出之臺海采風圖考中見之要其末句註

明鴉片土所出之咬𠺕吧即德國醫士甘伯佛耳書所言以阿片水調和黃烟

供人吸之閣婆也就甘伯佛耳書觀之可知黃烟爲鴉片前鋒引線矣臺灣乃

康熙年閒鄭成功盤踞之處於前明時止以淡水雞籠爲名國朝始呼爲臺灣

也當鄭成功據有之時中國人赴彼卽居者不乏而狡猾阨之往來貿易事未

嘗斷絶各地之無業流氓聚於彼而吸鴉片之汚俗亦卽與起於彼地矣

又臺灣志云鴉片烟不知始自何來煮以銅鍋烟筒如短棍無頑惡少羣夜飲

遂成風俗時以蜜糖諸品及鮮果十數碟佐之勸後來者初赴欲不用錢久則不

能自已傾家赴之矣能通宵不寐助淫慾始以爲樂後遂不可復救一日輟飲則

面皮頓縮脣齒露骹神欲驚復飲乃愈然三年之後無不死矣閩此爲救煕島

爽誑傾唐人財命者南洋諸島照中國爲藩鎮官滇愚夫不悟傳入中國已十餘

年廈門多有而臺灣特甚殊可哀也今臺灣人照內地亦曰唐山

當雍正年間此等喪人性命敗人名節駭人聽聞之吸鴉片事已入中國內地都

門亦有風聞直達宸聽是以大淸會典刑部兵律關津欵內定有云與販鴉片烟

照收買違禁貨物例枷號一月發近充軍如私開鴉片烟館引誘良家子弟者

照邪教惑衆律擬絞監侯爲從杖一百流三千里船戶地保鄉佑人等俱杖一百

徒三年如兵役人等藉端需索計贓照枉法律治罪失察之汎口地方文武各官

并不行監察之海關監督均交部嚴加議處雍正七年事也卽是條反覆推揣之

罪歸於與販者開館者隱惡不舉者并藉端需索者寡不疑及吸飲者豈以其死

期已兆卽蓋國家於吸食之人非視爲無罪乃以其三年必死刑罰已足奚必復

定斬絞軍流若等罪名哉

雍正八年擬定臺灣流寓之民凡無妻室者應逐令過水交原籍收管其有妻子

田產者如犯歐血訂盟誘番殺人捏造匿名揭帖強盜窩家造賣賭具應擬斬絞

軍流等條除本犯依律定擬外此內為從罪輕之人并教唆之訟師均應審明

逐令過水其越界生事之漢姦如在生番地方謀佔番田并勾串棍徒包攬偷渡

及販賣鴉片烟者亦分別治罪逐令過水見大清會典

自彼時以後鴉片在中國不惟充醫病之藥品兼為人日所吸食之物矣而販

賣者之禁令亦甚緊嚴矣因吸食鴉片生出之惡端甚多即以其所生各惡端

之大小而定其罪之重輕非緣都門輦轂下已有吸者觸目傷懷始立此禁也

其時北省尚無吸食者雍正皇帝之心中亦止知於福建省沿海之廈門等處

有此惡習開鴉片館者誘良家子弟名敗德應擬以罪狀其吸食者乃毀己

之身傾己之家喪已之命皇上見此等忘身忘家之徒不可不視同大罪人是

以言出惟行禁令嚴厲不慮及人之視同具文也

乾隆元年重修之雲南通志所載永昌府土產中亦有鴉片其時殆經回教人或

他等人帶種子至彼地彼地遂種植緣人多奉之為大力藥品并視為易售之貨

物也或由緬甸西藏等國陸路運進亦可上文己曾言及前明萬曆年間有人由

印度東哥羅滿得拉海濱之尼加巴得并米利亞布耳載鴉片出口赴緬甸暹邏

豈不可將罌粟種子由緬甸帶至雲南乎且雲南彼時種罌粟大抵仍以之充藥

品或亦似巴耳西亞按時喬服之陋俗耶

二十四

乾隆七年成之御纂醫宗金鑑中治肺氣虛損之人參養肺湯即以罌粟穀合人

參杏仁等十味爲一劑更有治湯火燒之罌粟膏用罌粟花十五朶無花以穀

代之其方歌曰　罌粟膏治湯火燒香油罌粟共熬白臘更兼真輕粉患處搽

塗痛即消　復有治癰疽疔毒之乳香黃者散其方歌曰　乳香黃者治氣癰癰

疽諸毒痛難富未成即消已成潰歸芍參者芎地黃乳沒罌粟甘草節更醫打撲

筋骨傷　猶有以罌粟穀合他藥醫病之數方姑不贅述

康熙初鴉片准作藥材進口每擔納稅銀三兩後又每包加稅銀二兩四分五

自禁開鴉片烟舘以來南省之沿海口岸仍屬奉鴉片爲藥品進口納稅（見海國圖志）

由印度運來之箱數歲歲增加屬於葡萄亞人經理雖於乾隆二十二年英國公

司已得有出鴉片之孟加拉地運來中國一事俞屬商人自辦至乾隆三十八年

英公司將此由來商人自辦納稅之土產歸爲國家自理之欵項乾隆四十六年

運來中國又歸英國公司掌管矣乾隆四十七年七月駐中國澳門理通商事務

之英國人函至英國總貿易公司者云阿片一貨中國之禁令極嚴搜查出鴉片

起於岸英燒載鴉片之船沒於官典販買之中國官之所以敢於販運華

民之所以敢於購買者由來仲仗中國官吏勠奉陰違牟利入己也故仍可或在

澳門或在黃埔進口起貨澳門雖歸葡萄亞人旅居而收規禮之權操自華人鴉

片離爲違禁貨物從無人犯事受罰信函中又云乾隆四十五年補授之兩廣總

督有居心廉潔守正不阿之名聞其宅心立志云有以鴉片進口之事告發者併

必嚴切根究按例懲辦見西愿之一千七百八十三年英國議政院特派巡查者

覆議政院之印度情形記第六本後附之七十七號信件片於乾隆三十四年時鴉片進口由二百箱漸增

至千箱總督之欲加嚴禁其有見於是歟　當夫乾隆十八年時也住廣東之英商曾將粵海關徵收各

貨稅則譯成西國文遍寄光緒八年某公於和蘭國書肆幸得其書內所載者即

乾隆十八年中國粵海關監督徵收船鈔并貨稅之一切例條其按類分列與現

時之稅則差無幾惟出口貨物不分為二欵所徵之稅項名目有五一

進口貨物照稅則徵收正稅二出口貨物并復出口運往寗波等處沿海口岸之

貨物俱有稅則且按照價值百兩者抽收銀六兩三為進出口貨物完納正稅外

所納之規費而此項分為二一為將餉銀解京之脚價抬費一為監督署上下人

役之茶飯銀而合計此二項規費援進口貨稅比較之幾及正稅銀數之半四為

船鈔五即額外餽贈之禮并將其時由北京戶部批准發予該海關照用之書籍

冊簿三件中摘譯數端更將其書中格式畧舉大義供人觀瞻一為抽收正稅則

例原康熙二十五年擬定不能妄有更改二為比例稅則即新來貨與舊貨較比

酌定抽收稅銀增訂之新例也如是擬訂之新例累至百有五十欵時咨部送戶

部核奪雍正十一年曾經部核准㽞此每歷三二年有一次將其情形咨部考核

續入比例稅則三為估價冊廣東省於徵收出口貨物之稅外俱以貨物值銀百

兩收取六兩爲例乾隆二十年時稅則鬻絲百斤估價百兩茶葉百斤估價八兩

白糖百斤估價一兩五錢紅糖百斤估價一兩冰糖百斤估價二兩五錢大黃百

斤估價一兩五錢麝香一斤估價一兩五錢鴉片一斤估價五錢而一箱鴉片大

抵值洋錢不足百圓富康熙二十五年時鴉片每斤納稅三分援估價之數計之

殆亦屬值百抽六也

乾隆五十七年英國欽使馬戛得尼至中國時有英人一名巴羅一名斯噹頓者

曾隨來中國回英國後將由津沽至北京并由陸路回至廣東途中所見聞詳細

記錄者欄印成書於論及天津至通州路途所見各種風俗中并曹居官之人眼

餘多吸黃烟嘗將香料攙入時或吸食鴉片未確言攙合黃烟與否且言伊等有

時將檳榔含浸口中

海國圖志中有云鴉片之鑠竹爲管就燃吸食蓋自乾隆末年始伊之爲是言也

或以吸食鴉片之俗風始傳至北京耳其書中并云嘉慶初奉旨禁止而廣東官

府仍准鴉片躉船常灣在黃埔距省有十二里及道光二年遂議定規銀每箱若

干自總督衙門以及水路文武官員皆有之惟關口所得最多或在船上來取或

在省城交收皆逐月交清亦有將鴉片准折每大自一箱至百五十箱不等者此

等走私之情形直至道光二十年始止也

植物名寶圖考中云按罌粟花唐以前不著錄開寶本草收入米穀下品宋時猶

罌粟湯但其殼粟功用僅止澀歛爲洩痢之藥明時一粒金丹多服爲害近來阿

芙蓉流毒天下與斷腸草無異然其罪不在花也列之羣芳

英國領事官施本君前駐劄於四川重慶府者也於光緒辛巳年嘗將中國西

南四省產之鴉片估其大數謂四川省歲產者本地人民約用五萬四千擔有

十二萬三千擔售與鄰省販運之東者卽七萬擔內有納稅者四萬走私者三

萬雲南省歲產三萬五千擔貴州省一萬擔湖北省二千擔四省共計歲產鴉

片二十二萬四千擔此該領事官約計四省所產之鴉片情形報與英國外務

衙門者也該衙門乃轉達至議政院刷印散發據彼四省歲產鴉片二十二萬

擔之數與壬午年由印度運來六萬六千九百擔較比之幾多及三倍矣況中

國他省猶有產鴉片者乎